A  W O R D

*to the*

W I S E

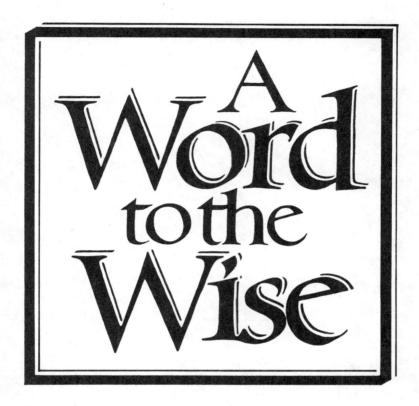

# A Word to the Wise

HUDSON · T · ARMERDING

Tyndale House
Publishers, Inc.
Wheaton, Illinois

PHOTOS COURTESY OF
WHEATON COLLEGE
DOUGLAS GILBERT, PAGE 13
DON WORKMAN, PAGES 18, 24, 40
ROBERT MCKENDRICK, PAGE 76
JIM WHITMER, PAGE 124


ALL SCRIPTURE REFERENCES ARE TAKEN FROM
THE KING JAMES VERSION OF THE BIBLE,
UNLESS OTHERWISE NOTED.

LIBRARY OF CONGRESS CATALOG CARD NUMBER 80-50664
ISBN 0-8423-0099-6
COPYRIGHT © 1980 BY HUDSON T. ARMERDING
ALL RIGHTS RESERVED
FIRST PRINTING, AUGUST 1980
PRINTED IN THE UNITED STATES OF AMERICA

*To the many*
*Brave Sons and Daughters True*
*whose lives and ministry*
*reflect the wisdom from above*
*and eloquently testify*
*to their commitment*
*for Christ and His Kingdom.*
*H.T.A.*

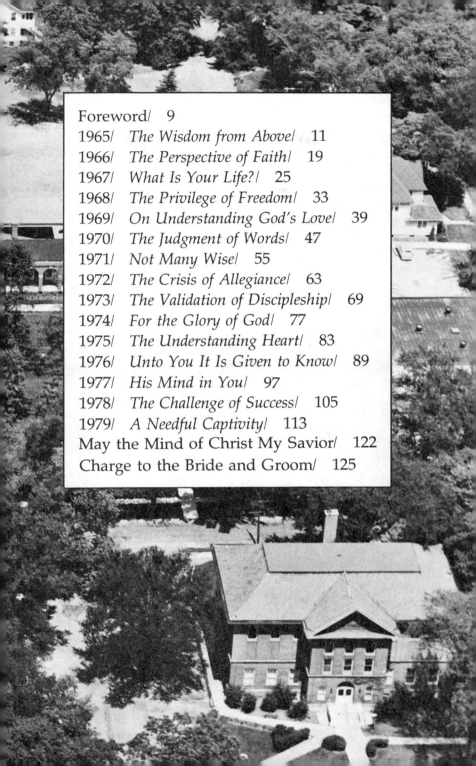

*Dr. Billy Graham with A. Harold Anderson, president of J. Emil Anderson and Sons, Inc., in front of the Billy Graham Center, under construction.*

# A Word
# about the
# Author

My warm association with Dr. Hudson T. Amerding dates back to our collegiate days on the Wheaton College campus where Ruth and I both knew him as an upperclassman. Even then he was an excellent student, active in the Men's Glee Club, and busy in the affairs of his Literary Society and of his class. I have watched his commitment to Biblical truth as well as to excellence in academic endeavor in his roles both as a faculty member and as an administrator at two Christian colleges, one in New England, and later at Wheaton College. Both Ruth and I have been pleased for a number of years to serve on the Board of Trustees at Wheaton where we have had good opportunity to know this brother in Christ and to see how he thinks and works.

He is an articulate person in setting forth ideas in his writings as well as in speaking and has been gifted to convey truth with the fresh impact of language free of cliches. As one who welcomes new insights on old questions, he takes the clear teaching of God's Word as itself authoritative in all that it affirms, and acts accordingly. I have been present for some of these occasions when the baccalaureate messages were given and know firsthand something of the impact made by these timely topics on the hearers, both students and parents.

A review of the subject matter of the ensuing chapters is a commentary on the times represented in that period from 1965 to the present when the youth of our nation and our world were buffeted by tragic war, social change, and uncertain voices calling for allegiance. Through this period of cultural upheaval, these messages to graduating seniors, anchored by the principles taught in the Scriptures, sought to provide a strong basis for faith, hope, and reason for the young Christians entering a secularized and largely unfriendly world to find their places of service. Because I know and commend the author, it is easy for me to commend his writings. May God bless its reading for your heart's good and the glory of our Lord Jesus Christ.

*Billy Graham*
April 1980

# 1965
## *The Wisdom from Above*

"WHO is a wise man and endued with knowledge among you?" This question from the Epistle of James contains two words that merit definition because they help us to understand whether or not we indeed belong within the classification which the Apostle James had in mind.

The first word is *wisdom*. Dr. A. T. Robertson suggests that this is one of the most felicitous words used to describe the highest of intellectual achievements. It is clear, therefore, that superior intellectual achievement is not to be shunned by the Christian. Instead, it is something earnestly to be desired. This word is used when the Apostle James, in the first chapter of his epistle, speaks of men asking wisdom of God. It is also used with respect to that which characterizes our Lord Jesus Christ. The Apostle Paul, when speaking of the Savior in 1 Corinthians 1:24, describes Christ as "the power of God, and the wisdom of God." In Colossians 2:2, 3 he speaks of Christ "in whom are hid all the treasures of wisdom and knowledge." And again in verse 9 he reinforces this by saying that in the Lord Jesus there is located all the fulness of the Godhead in bodily form. These Scriptures make clear that our Lord Jesus Christ, even in his incarnate ministry, had the wisdom and knowledge characteristic of deity.

11

Specifically, Christ is vitally related to the various areas of knowledge or of wisdom with which we are familiar. The Apostle Paul, in Romans 1:20, speaks about one of these when he says: "For the invisible things of him from the creation of the world are clearly seen, being understood by the things which are made, even his eternal power and Godhead; so that they are without excuse." In Romans 2:15 he indicates another area when he remarks that the Gentiles, which have not the law, show the work of the law written in their hearts with their consciences bearing witness to this. And then in Romans 3:2, the Apostle Paul commends the Jewish Christians because to them are committed the oracles of God, the written revelation.

Whether it be that phenomenal knowledge which we may observe and classify, or that subjective knowledge which Dr. J. Edwin Orr calls "the universal intuition," or the Word of God written, the Savior relates to each of these. Hebrews 1 tells us that it was by the Son that the worlds were created, and the thought is expressed by the Apostle Paul in the first chapter of Colossians. John in his Gospel speaks of the fact that this One in coming into the world lighted every man. In Matthew 5:17, the Lord Jesus said that he did not come to destroy the law and the prophets, but to fulfill them.

From this we should not infer that the Savior's relationship to knowledge is equally significant for all men. There is a unique way in which this is true for Christians. In 1 Corinthians 1:30, the Apostle says: "But of him are ye in Christ Jesus, who of God is made unto us wisdom, and righteousness, and sanctification, and redemption." By the marvelous transformation which takes place in our hearts and lives through faith in Jesus Christ, we have had placed within us the very life of Christ, and therefore we are now able to think God's thoughts after him. We have the capacity to know and understand his revelation. By this same regeneration, we have been given the Holy Spirit as our teacher and guide. Thus this word of wisdom has particular significance for us. The term *wisdom* relates to a person who does more than simply recog-

12

*Dr. Hudson Taylor Armerding, president of Wheaton College.*

nize the hand of God in nature and in man, or even with respectful admiration in Holy Scripture. Through saving faith in Christ, he has been born again as a child of God.

The other word used in the question posed by the Apostle James is *knowledge*. This term occurs only here in the New Testament. It describes that person who has the knowledge or experience of an expert. We recognize this kind of knowledge on the athletic field, in the musical world, and in other areas of skill. The word describes a Christian who has not only propositional knowledge concerning Christianity but also experiential knowledge, one who has tested and proved the great promises of God and found them to be "yea and amen." To identify such a person, the Apostle James suggests a test —a proper test in my opinion, because today so very often we fall short by being satisfied simply to know. Rather there should be a tangible demonstration in the spirit of meekness.

This is consistent with the Apostle James's stress on works. It also concurs with the Apostle Paul's statement in Ephesians 2, that we are created in Christ Jesus unto good works, and with the Apostle Peter's exhortation in his second epistle, chapter 2, to mix with our faith virtue and knowledge and all the rest. So this emphasis is not unique to James; it is part of the basic fabric of the New Testament.

The Apostle James continues by identifying two alternatives. Some may think that Christians are not free to select a negative option, but I find this taught throughout Scripture. For example, in the Epistle to the Galatians, Paul sets forth the alternatives of law and grace, that of being a servant or a son, of sowing to the flesh or sowing to the Spirit. Similarly, James sets forth two alternatives. There is first of all a wisdom which is not of God. It is possible even as Christians to pursue this kind of wisdom. James describes it as earthly and natural and devilish. The term *earthly* might include such a position as logical positivism; *natural* might incorporate certain kinds of existentialism; and *devilish* might refer to the questioning of the validity of Holy Scripture and the commandments of God.

This wisdom is circumscribed, is often intensely personal, and may be induced by the enemy of our souls, but has an inevitable outcome. The King James Version says: "If ye have bitter envying and strife in your hearts. . . ." It could be expressed this way: "If you have a harsh zeal to promote your own viewpoint. . . ."

One commentator has said that this was the kind of situation in which a very brilliant person with splendid natural abilities and training was so prone to insist upon his own point of view as to discredit completely those with whom he did not agree. John Calvin, in his commentary, says that what James had in mind was the pagan philosopher who was out to destroy the person with whom he disagreed, to denigrate his reputation and to use the pitiless strength of logic to reduce him to impotence. It is possible for the intellectually gifted Christian, with the brilliance he possesses and the unusual facility with concepts and words that he has, to fall prey to this alternative: to use his exceptional insight to bring someone to confusion and embarrassment, to be intolerant of those who have not had the privileges he has had, to seek to be one who would advance his own cause at the expense of others. Scripture says that for such a person the end product is confusion and every evil work.

I am persuaded that much of the confusion and conflict which besets the Christian church today is not due to great issues of theology. Instead, it is because brilliant leaders have not been willing to act with meekness. Instead they have gained a following, and then, to maintain this following, have felt obliged to discredit those who would oppose them.

The other alternative is beautiful. It has the seven qualities of that wisdom which is from above and refers especially to our Lord Jesus Christ. To my mind, when one studies the person and work of the Savior, he is able to find a practical illustration of the wisdom which is pure, peaceable, gentle, easy to be entreated, without partiality, without hypocrisy, and full of good fruits. This is our Lord Jesus Christ.

When you have these alternatives before you, either of giving way and committing yourself to that wisdom which is earthly, natural, and devilish, or to that wisdom which is from above, the real issue is one of sovereignty. I think of an illustration in the Old Testament of a man who had extraordinary brilliance; in fact, Scripture speaks of Solomon as one before whom there was none such and after whom there would be none such again. Yet despite his capabilities and insights he did not use these to advantage and failed miserably.

By contrast, consider the Apostle Paul, one of the most gifted of all the New Testament apostles. In 2 Corinthians 12, he tells us his story: he says that because of the abundance of the revelations he had experienced "there was given to me a thorn in the flesh . . .lest I should be exalted above measure." It may have been this that prompted him to write in 1 Corinthians 1: "For [you] see your calling, brethren, how that not many wise . . .not many mighty, not many noble are called," and then to remark that God has chosen the foolish things of the world, the base things of the world, the things which are not, so that no flesh should glory in his presence. So when we are faced with these alternatives, the Lord warns us not to choose to exalt ourselves and thus diminish in any particular the honor, the glory, and the praise which belong to him. That is why I believe it is a question of sovereignty.

By way of illustration, consider this experience of a friend of mine. He was counseling with a young woman who formerly had confessed to being a Christian. As she sat in his living room she said she was no longer a Christian, and then told him and his wife that she wanted to be free to be immoral, to indulge in drunkenness, to do things which would be a shock to her culture and her friends. After about three hours of conversation, my friend asked her, "What is your real problem?" She replied, "Aren't you shocked by what I've said?" He answered, "No, and I want you to know that in spite of what you have told us, we love you in the Lord and we earnestly desire your best welfare." Her reply was significant: "To answer your question, the problem is that Jesus Christ wants sovereignty over all of my life, and I am not prepared to give him that sovereignty."

The Lord Jesus says to us as he did to his hearers long ago, "Come unto me all ye that labour and are heavy laden, and I will give you rest. Take my yoke upon you, and learn of me; for I am meek and lowly in heart: and ye shall find rest unto your souls" (Matt. 11:28, 29). Was there any person in all of the universe who better deserved honor and exalted status than our Lord Jesus Christ? It is this One who asks us to have his yoke placed upon us. I envision it as if Jesus Christ were placing himself in one side of his yoke and saying to the Christian, "Place yourself in the other side of this yoke and then learn of me—where I go, you go; the direction I take, you take; learn of me, for I am meek and lowly in heart."

This applies directly to James's statement: "Who is a wise man and endued with knowledge among you? Let him shew out of a good manner of life his works with meekness of wisdom." With this kind of wisdom and knowledge we may enter upon our chosen field of service and there find satisfaction and blessing, together with the tranquility of one who is subordinated to the yoke of Jesus Christ.

# 1966
# *The Perspective of Faith*

UNITY remains one of mankind's unfulfilled ambitions. If anything, the divisions seem sharper and the antipathies more profound than ever. Whether in the economic, political, racial, or social realms, there is a polarization that at times erupts into bitterness and strife. Apparently the adversary role is considered appropriate if not inevitable.

This point of view has had its impact on family life and Christian fellowship. It has become fashionable to suggest that discontinuity (or the "gap," as it is popularly known) is inherent between the generations and, for whatever reasons, between Christians.

When such an assertion is viewed in the light of Christian revelation, however, it is immediately apparent that what the Word of God teaches is not in agreement with the idea of discontinuity. This distinction is graphically illustrated by the two ordinances or practices of the Church, Baptism and the Lord's Supper.

However we may differ as to the mode of baptism, it is generally agreed that it is a sign of our identification with Christ. When the Bible speaks of the unity of the body of Christ, the term *baptism* is used: "For by one Spirit are we all baptized into one body." It is clear then that baptism, whether

19

by outward sign or the mystical action of the Holy Spirit, identifies us not only with our Savior but also with one another. In fact, the relationship of individual believers in the body of Christ is the kind of unity that makes possible true spiritual communication.

The other observance of the Church which is predicated on relationship is the Lord's Supper. Scripture describes this as "communion." This is because "we being many are one bread and one body: for we are all partakers of that one bread." Every time the Lord's Supper is celebrated, there is not only a declaration of the Lord's death but also an affirmation of the Christian's vital relationship to Christ and because of this to other believers.

These practices of the Church are consistent with the biblical truths about our conversion and its effects on us. The Apostle Peter speaks of our being born again, not of corruptible seed, but of incorruptible, by the Word of God which lives and abides forever. That such an experience brings us into a right relationship to God is expressed in Galatians: "For ye are all the children of God by faith in Christ Jesus." By regeneration, therefore, we are made part of the family of God, having been born into it through God's gracious provision for us in salvation.

All those who enjoy this status have the Holy Spirit. The Apostle Paul declares that if any man have not the Spirit of Christ, he is none of his. The presence and ministry of the Holy Spirit are of great significance in the consideration of the problem of an individual's communication with God and with his fellow believers. When the Lord Jesus was here on earth, he promised that "when he, the Spirit of truth, is come, he will guide you into all truth. . . ." The same thought is expressed by the Apostle Paul in 1 Corinthians: "Now we have received, not the spirit of the world, but the spirit which is of God; that we might know the things that are freely given to us of God."

The Christian Church, then, has one truth, the revelation of God, and one means of knowing that truth, the Holy Spirit.

Moreover, this unity applies to all who are a part of the body of Christ, whatever their economic, social, or cultural status.

Now the significance of this unity is not limited to those who make up the Church in the world today. The writer of Hebrews describes the Christians of his time as being surrounded by a great cloud of witnesses. It is generally agreed that these are the men and women described in chapter 11. Since they had already died, the question is how the Christians of a later time could be surrounded by such a cloud of witnesses. At this point the term "compassed about" is of importance in understanding the relationship between the people of God in a previous era and those of the present generation. This same term was used by the Lord Jesus when he said of those who cause one of God's little ones to stumble, that it would be better if a millstone were hung about (or "compassed about") their necks. In Acts the Apostle Paul employed the same word when he spoke of his being "bound" with a chain. Perhaps the most illustrative of all the usages is found in Hebrews where the earthly high priest is described as being compassed with infirmity. Each of these references suggests a close contiguity which, particularly in the case of the earthly high priest, involves his basic characteristics as a human being.

This intimacy of association is true of our spiritual linkage with the body of believers of other eras. To understand the significance of this, consider the statement in Hebrews 11: "And these all, having obtained a good report through faith, received not the promise: God having provided some better thing for us, that they without us should not be made perfect."

The concept of perfection or completeness is well illustrated by the other Scriptures where this same term is used to describe the earthly ministry of the Lord Jesus. We are told that the Savior, through his earthly experience, was made perfect or complete. When this is applied to the body of Christ, composed of believers of all ages, the experiences of those of one era make a vital contribution to the completeness of the whole body of Christ. It is possible that the Apostle Paul had this in mind when he said, "who now rejoice in my sufferings for you, and fill up that which is behind of the afflictions of Christ in my flesh for his body's sake, which is the church."

Here it is pertinent to consider the Apostle Peter's statement that Christ has left us an example that we should follow his steps. There has been much misuse of the exhortation to follow the example of the Lord Jesus. Some have been urged to follow Christ's example before they have ever come to him in saving faith. The Apostle Peter declares precisely the opposite. Those who by saving faith in Christ have new life are after that enjoined to exemplify in their own lives, as they react to suffering and rejection, what was the experience of the Savior himself.

This is the intent in Hebrews 12: "Looking unto Jesus the author and finisher of our faith, who for the joy that was set before him endured the cross, despising the shame, and is set down at the right hand of the throne of God." We are urged to consider him who endured such contradiction of sinners against himself lest we be wearied and faint in our minds. One purpose of this is to fulfill our responsibility to other generations of believers by living lives of moral rectitude and of obedience in the face of suffering as we manifest our devotion to the Savior.

In achieving this, one of the remarkable resources of the Christian—not to be found in the lives of so many of his contemporaries—is his perspective. For most of the world today, they would rather not contemplate the future; or if they do take time to ponder it, they can see nothing but confusion and the obscuring of any clear way. Such is not the situation as far as the Christian is concerned. He is not only able, by the eye of faith, to look to Jesus as the originator and the completer of his faith, but is also able to recognize, in the vast sweep of God's work in the world, the pattern which is moving toward the consummation of all things. Through the difficulties and trials of this age, the Christian waits with anticipation the return of God's Son from heaven. It is constructive in this connection to note that the anticipation of his return is a purifying hope. So once again the development of a true Christian perspective, in all of its eschatological dimensions, has as its practical outgrowth a life of holiness and purity, which in itself stands in stark contrast to the profligacy of the present age.

We who are part of the body of Christ must make our distinctive contribution to the completeness of the Church as a tangible evidence of our unity with other believers. This will demand of us the highest moral and ethical resolution and a life that is lived in consistency with the Word of God and in anticipation of the imminent return of Jesus Christ. In discharging this responsibility we do not stand alone. We have not only the inspiration of the saints and heroes of the past but also the indwelling presence and power of the Holy Spirit and the strength and encouragement of today's Church. As we are obedient to the declared principles of Scripture, we may confidently expect that the resources of God Almighty himself will be provided to enable us to live lives worthy of him. In so doing, we will in ourselves become an inspiration to our generation and those which are to follow us as the Lord tarries. Added to this, we will fulfill his prayer, "That they all may be one."

Let us be found faithful in this task. As we do so we will learn with new appreciation the pertinence of this promise in Hebrews: "Wherefore we receiving a kingdom which cannot be moved, let us have grace, whereby we may serve God acceptably with reverence and godly fear: for our God is a consuming fire."

# 1967
# *What Is*
# *Your Life?*

SOMETIMES the fear is voiced that evangelicals are not asking the right questions. While on occasion this concern may be justified, there are scriptural inquiries that are timeless in their relevance and should be asked of every generation. One of these is, "What shall it profit a man if he shall gain the whole world and lose his own soul or what shall a man give in exchange for his soul?" Another is, "From whence come wars and fightings among you?" The Apostle James's answer to this inquiry provides the context for the question he subsequently poses, "What is your life?"

To understand the significance of this question it is necessary to take into account the Apostle's discussion of the previous one. He makes clear that the source of personal and corporate strife is found in the selfish desires of mankind. These have caused men to be governed by their passions, dominated by Satan, and controlled by a world system which seeks to subordinate God's laws to its own judgment.

In contrast to this, Christians are urged by the Apostle to acknowledge the sovereignty of God over every aspect of their lives. This requires an act of the will in repudiation of all that would in any way tend to create a divided loyalty and ultimately disobedience. Throughout, there is the assurance that such a choice makes possible a manner of life which can be successfully lived out in experience. And so the answer to the question "What is your life?" is directly related to the matter of personal decision.

The importance of this is emphasized by an illustration. James cites a manner of life common in the Apostle's day and in ours as well. This is a practical atheism which obviously considers God irrelevant to the plans being laid for successful business enterprise. An illustration from another dimension of human experience would be equally pertinent, for in discussing future plans mankind generally takes into account the desirable goals and even on occasion the circumstantial hazards (witness the habit of insuring a venture) but seldom if ever the prospect of the intervention of God. This is left to the description after the fact of "acts of God" which are uniformly catastrophic. Any *beneficial* results are perceived to be purely human.

Furthermore, the focus of attention seems to center on monetary gain. Repeatedly, no other values are cited. Thus, practical materialism accompanies practical atheism. This characterizes the present age whether the political ideology be communist or capitalist. The indictment is greater, however, as far as the Western democracies are concerned; for we—in our better moments—affirm values that are not simply material and classify "things" as means rather than ends. Yet we cannot escape the pertinence of James's illustration. It is reflected in our publications and in our daily conversation and correspondence.

We are not to infer from the Apostle's statement that all planning for the future is wrong or that material things are to be despised. The other teachings in this same epistle having to do with provision for one's household would make such conclusions invalid. It is simply that the planning for and use of one's material means must essentially include rather than ignore God's sovereignty.

Failure to do this may be seen in the account of the rich man and Lazarus. The rich man enjoyed a measurable degree of material prosperity but obedience to God was not part of his success story. The ultimate assessment of his life was tragic and terribly final. Furthermore, there was no opportunity to correct matters, even on behalf of others. The same was true of the children of Israel who placed physical safety from the formidable inhabitants of the promised land ahead of doing the will of God. With the exception of Caleb and Joshua—the dissenting minority—they all perished in the wilderness.

The foolishness of planning without taking into account the will of God basically locates in the inherent limitations of man's knowledge of the future. He may speculate but he cannot ever really know what will happen.

This is the significance of the word James uses to indicate man's inability to know what is in the future. It is a term for knowledge about the details of a particular circumstance. The force of the statement is that human beings do not have the remotest idea what may take place in the future.

There is an illustration of this in the experience of Abraham. Scripture says that he went out not knowing where he went. The reason God honored him was because of his faith, not his foreknowledge. In fact, the instances in which Abraham sought to exercise his prescience do nothing to enhance his reputation but rather exhibit the finiteness of even this great man of God. The writer of Proverbs properly sums up the matter by saying, "Boast not thyself of tomorrow, for thou knowest not what a day may bring forth."

This is true not only of circumstance, however, but also of our earthly existence as well. This is the significance of the question, "What is your life?" From the context it is clear that James is not speaking of a quality of life but its duration in this scene. The word that he used for "life" is one which is often employed in the New Testament to describe the life of the risen Savior or that of God himself as well as the eternal life granted to all who are redeemed.

The uncertainty of how long we shall live is illustrated by the Apostle's comparison of this to a vapor. Its visibility is brief and its duration limited. So it is with human life. Even those who recognize that there will be an ultimate time of reckoning cannot overcome the inherent limitation on their knowledge of how long they will live. So it is necessary to accept the fact of life's uncertainty and to acknowledge God's sovereignty over its duration here on earth.

This is the point of the Apostle's exhortation, "For ye ought to say, If the Lord will." Any declaration of intent on the part of the Christian should be expressed, either explicitly or implicitly, by this phrase. These words, reportedly used by the Greeks before beginning any undertaking, were once a common expression among God's people. Thomas Fuller, in *Good Thoughts in Bad Times,* has said of the interjection of this expression into his writings, "Let critics censure it for bad grammar. I am sure it is good divinity." Yet admittedly it can become a meaningless verbal talisman, having no vital connection with our attitudes or practices. Such is not the intent of the Apostle's statement. It should be an affirmation which acknowledges God's sovereign wisdom and power, a confessing once for all that personal desires or ambitions are of less consequence than the will of God.

Furthermore, it is essential to recognize that life itself is also only by the will of God. Fortunate indeed are those who have gladly accepted this and rejoice in it. Conceivably such a one was Enoch. His recorded life span was much shorter than that of his contemporaries; but he is celebrated in the history of the believing community as one who walked with God and was not, for *God took him.* Nor is Enoch an isolated illustration. In more modern times there have been those who in the estimation of their contemporaries came to an untimely end. Jim Elliot and Ed McCully, the Auca missionary martyrs, died when they were still young men; but it can be said of them that they walked with God. Equally it can be affirmed that they "were not; for God took them." This was because they were living in the will of God, not just subject to the fateful accidents of capricious circumstance.

It is only natural for us to consider human life—particularly our own—to be precious and to seek to extend its duration. Yet even this may not be for our best interest nor that of those who follow us. When he was at the point of death, Hezekiah pleaded with God for healing and as a result had his life extended fifteen years. From the Scripture we know that he erred later in showing the treasures of his kingdom to those who were really his enemies. He may well have suffered remorse as he reflected on his foolish action. But even more significant is the record of his son's calculated disobedience which repeatedly was cited as the cause of God's later judgment. The striking statistic is that Manasseh was twelve years old when he succeeded his father on the throne. This son, born in the extension of time given Hezekiah, did irreparable harm to the cause of God's people. We can only surmise that it would have been far better for Hezekiah and his kingdom had he died rather than lived the additional fifteen years. To the knowledgeable soul it is always true: God's time is best.

Within our earthly life span, however, we are obliged to act as well as exist. The urge toward activism, so characteristic of our age, makes us impatient of any restraint beyond that of our own decision. Yet, just as we should acknowledge God's sovereignty over our continued existence in this life, so we should acknowledge his sovereignty over *what* we do. Scripture here is not precise, simply because all of life should be recognized as under the control of God—material, social, spiritual. So the Apostle Paul could say, "Whatsoever ye do in word or deed, do all in the name of the Lord Jesus, giving thanks to God and the Father by him."

The emphasis of the statement is, however, that only by the sovereign will of God are we given *opportunity* to do, as far as the future is concerned. There is not in question the details as to *what* we are to do. The prescriptions of the Word of God and the subjective leading of the Holy Spirit, as well as the circumstantial ordering of events, are furnished to us for those times of decision made possible in the opportunities graciously provided in the will of God.

That God orders the course of history is a concept generally accepted by the religious community. Periodically there are pivotal happenings which illustrate forcefully his sovereignty over the affairs of men.

In 1942 in the Pacific Ocean west of Midway Island, there took place an encounter which in retrospect was one of the key battles of the Second World War. In the United States Naval Institute Proceedings for June 1967, Lieutenant Commander Thomas E. Powers, an instructor at the United States Naval Academy, wrote an essay entitled "Incredible Midway." In commenting on the essay the editor says, "A sophisticated reader would reject as absurd a work of fiction the plot of which hinged on circumstances and events similar to those surrounding the Battle of Midway. He doubtless would dismiss the story as too contrived, too bizarre to have ever happened. Yet, of course, it did happen."

Commander Powers recounts how the Japanese submarines, ordered to intercept units of the United States fleet leaving Pearl Harbor, arrived on station two days late, being delayed by overhaul repairs. Had they been on schedule, they might have attacked some of the units later involved at Midway. As it was, these ships had already passed them by.

On the morning of June 4, Admiral Nagumo ordered search planes launched from the heavy cruiser *Tone.* Due to catapult problems, one of the planes was launched a half hour behind schedule. Meanwhile, the Japanese admiral, convinced that a bombing attack against the island of Midway was necessary, ordered the carrier crews to change the armament of the aircraft from torpedoes to bombs. While this was in process, the plane which had been launched late found the American fleet. On hearing the report of the sighting, Admiral Nagumo ordered the aircraft rearmed with torpedoes. To comply, the crews were forced to stack the unloaded bombs in the open.

Had the sighting been even one half hour earlier the necessary changes in armament would have been far less extensive.

Later in the morning the United States torpedo planes attacked the Japanese formation just at the time the carrier decks were loaded with fully armed and fueled aircraft. The Japanese put up a spectacular defense against the low-flying aircraft, with the attention of even the lookouts being distracted and the defensive air patrol drawn down to the water's edge. At this instant, dive bombers from the United States fleet struck the carriers. The resulting fires ignited the closely packed aircraft, exploded the bombs stacked in the open, and eventually caused the sinking of three carriers. A fourth suffered a similar fate later in the day.

The author of the essay speaks of "luck" and "fate." To the Christian, the almost incredible progression of circumstances suggests the governing providence of a sovereign God in this strategic action. Yet our concern often is less with major circumstances such as these than with those happenings which directly affect our lives personally and about which we are obliged to make decisions.

Perhaps no more graphic illustration of the sovereignty of the will of God in an individual life can be seen than in the earthly ministry of our Lord Jesus Christ. Compared to the biblical three score years and ten, his earthly life was brief. Even more so was his public ministry as contrasted with, for example, the kingship of David. Moreover, we learn from the Savior's experience that doing the will of God may be a formidable experience and terribly costly. How magnificent, in the light of this, are the words uttered in the garden, "Nevertheless not my will, but thine, be done." The writer of Hebrews has captured the true significance of Calvary for our Savior: " . . .who for the joy that was set before him endured the cross, despising the shame, . . ." In Christ were combined an understanding of the purposes of God for the world and the ordering of his earthly ministry in the light of those purposes.

31

Jesus Christ remarkably transcends every generation gap and is a model appropriate for every Christian of any age, including ours. Thus, while acknowledging the fact that our earthly existence is, humanly speaking, uncertain and brief —a fact that we must confront—we can also reply to the question "What is your life?" in the words of the Apostle Paul, "To me to live is Christ." That being so, we can respond to the exhortation, "Let this mind be in you which was also in Christ Jesus," and permit him to be sovereign over our minds as well as over our circumstances and our destiny.

"What is your life?" Today it is as yet unjudged. Splendid predictions may have been made about us, but they remain speculative and will soon be forgotten unless actualized in the demanding rigor of our experience in the days to come. And our achievements are not subject alone to the evaluation of history. Ultimately in eternity we will come under the searching appraisal of God himself. His evaluation of our lives will be governed by the principle enunciated by James: "Therefore, to him that knoweth to do good, and doeth it not, to him it is sin."

Let it be our prayer that we may have the wisdom and the humility to confess with conviction, "If the Lord will, we shall live, and do this, or that." In biblical terms we will then enjoy true success and merit the "well done" of our Lord and Master, having learned that "the fear of the Lord is the beginning of wisdom."

# 1968
## *The Privilege of Freedom*

JEAN JACQUES ROUSSEAU began his famous work *The Social Contract* by saying, "Man is born free, and everywhere he is in chains. How has this change come about?" Perhaps there is no time in history when this question is being asked more frequently than today. The issue of man's freedom concerns the economist, the social scientist, the philosopher, and the theologian. It is also one of the major themes of the Bible.

When the commandment was given in Genesis 2 about the tree of the knowledge of good and evil, man had to decide whether or not he would obey. In a mistaken endeavor to attain even greater freedom or discretion, he succumbed to temptation. He believed Satan's lie that God by his commandment was denying him the prerogative of becoming as a god, knowing good and evil. And thus in his effort to attain greater freedom he lost his liberty to do what was pleasing to God because of the blighting effects of sin.

Man's subsequent history eloquently testifies to this inability, but his recurrent failures were assuredly not because of ignorance. To his chosen people God gave his Word; yet the Old Testament record is replete with accounts of the chronic disobedience of the children of Israel. They demonstrated clearly that even the most favored persistently fall short of

God's standards of performance. But neither can the rest of mankind plead ignorance. In Romans 2 Paul states that the Gentiles who do not have the biblical revelation yet have the law of God written on their hearts, to which their conscience bears witness. The result is that the individual's assessment of his behavior is either an accusation or an excuse. Thus man is aware of his dilemma in attempting to choose to do what is right as he exercises a supposed freedom.

This issue continues to trouble man. The existentialist Jean-Paul Sartre, in *Being and Nothingness,* said, "Man does not exist *first* in order to be free *subsequently;* there is no difference between the being of man and his *being free*." And in his book *Anti-Semitism and the Jew,* he said the authentic exercise of freedom might be with humiliation or horror and hate. Yet he insisted that *man was not free to cease being free,* despite these consequences.

Dr. Kurt Glaser, professor of Government at Southern Illinois University and a German scholar, has commented on one of the spokesmen for the New Left, Rudi Dutschke. He said this man exemplified his cause very well because he was caught up in the *process* of revolution and would be bored and disillusioned if a classless society was really achieved. The modern revolutionary may insist that of all men he is the most free, but in reality he is a captive of the circumstances in which he is involved and escapes only by suicide.

Against this somber background, the Christian gospel stands as the only way for man to achieve true freedom. The Apostle Paul spoke of Jesus Christ as commissioned by God to enter into history, identify with man's circumstances, and ultimately to encounter death. Because of this, he has appeared to some to be trapped in the same dilemma as the rest of mankind, but our Lord Jesus Christ was not as all other men are, for he could say, "I have power to lay down my life and I have power to take it again." He was not subject to sin and he was truly free to make decisions that were consistent with the will of God for the redemption of sinful man. Thus as the true

Liberator, the Lord Jesus secured deliverance for mankind from the confines of their sinful condition that historically made them incapable of doing the will of God.

The primacy of this liberation is crucial to the believer's manner of life. Even in the Christian world there is sometimes a tendency to invert the biblical sequence of freedom. Individuals are urged to make choices and decisions before they are liberated through salvation. Redemption not only includes the forgiveness of sin and the bestowal of eternal life, but also makes provision whereby man can have the ability to make decisions consonant with the will of God.

Thomas Huxley, the nineteenth-century biologist, philosopher, and thinker, on one occasion said, "The only freedom I care about is the freedom to do right; the freedom to do wrong I am ready to part with." Huxley's concern is that which the Christian gospel has brought to the redeemed community: the freedom to do right. This does not mean there will be no wrong decisions from now on. Instead it means that the Christian has an opportunity to choose whether to do the will of God or not and to be aware of the consequences. The Word of God says, "Be not deceived: God is not mocked; for whatsoever a man soweth, that shall he also reap. For he that soweth to his flesh shall of the flesh reap corruption; but he that soweth to the Spirit shall of the Spirit reap life everlasting" (Gal. 6:7, 8). With the privilege of choice comes the responsibility of decision. This cannot be avoided.

Consider the experience of the children of Israel. The writer of Hebrews says of them, "They could not enter in because of unbelief." They chose to reject the commandment of God and suffered the consequences. Similarly, Esau despised his birthright and then found no place of repentance though he sought it diligently with tears.

But some may ask whether subordination to the will of God eliminates the possibility of personal freedom of action. This matter is discussed by A. A. Hodge in his *Popular Lectures on Theological Themes*. By way of explanation he used an illustration of two ships at sea. One is without a rudder. It might be called a free vessel but actually is at the mercy of the wind and the currents, and so drifts helplessly to and fro. The other ship has a rudder and goes where the commanding officer of the vessel directs it. Clearly the ship which has a rudder and can be steered in a purposeful way is really free.

Sir William Blackstone in his *Commentaries on the Laws of England* cited the laws of nature to make the same point. He said that all creatures depend for their very existence on obedience to the laws or rules laid down by the Creator.

So it is with the Christian. The condition that governs his freedom to do the will of God is commitment, and the means whereby freedom through commitment may be enjoyed is through discipline. The Apostle Paul testified, "But I keep under my body, and bring it into subjection: lest that by any means, when I have preached to others I myself should be a castaway" (1 Cor. 9:27). This does not negate freedom. It simply means that by the practice of holiness we are able to have privileges which are denied to those who refuse this discipline. For example, how wonderfully free is the person who enters into marriage with a life unsullied by immorality. How free is that person who lives in a community without fear that some day he will be exposed because of unethical behavior.

There is another aspect of the privilege of freedom that is very important. Many in our time have committed themselves to causes that are antithetical to Christianity and have unquestionably served with extraordinary devotion. There are, for example, those in totalitarian systems who have voluntarily laid down their lives for their political beliefs. This is all the more remarkable when we remember that they have given themselves to a cause that has no assured outcome. It is impossible for them to know whether the sacrifice of their lives will ultimately produce the results they so desperately seek.

But when one exercises the privilege of freedom as a disciple of Jesus Christ, he can know with assurance that he is committed to a program that has significance for both time and eternity. This perspective ennobles his service and makes it truly meaningful and significant. The Apostle Paul expressed it this way: "Therefore, my beloved brethren, be ye stedfast, unmoveable, always abounding in the work of the Lord, forasmuch as ye know that your labour is not in vain in the Lord" (1 Cor. 15:58).

God in his redemptive mercy has made provision for our freedom from the bondage of a sinful condition. Being free we are now able to choose the good and the right. God gives us the privilege of freedom to do what the Apostle Paul has urged: "I beseech you therefore, brethren, by the mercies of God, that ye present your bodies a living sacrifice." This is not a negation of our freedom. It is rather the threshold through which we can enter into that liberty of which the Epistle to the Romans speaks: "But now being made free from sin, and become servants to God, ye have your fruit unto holiness, and the end everlasting life."

# 1969
## *On Understanding God's Love*

IN PREVIOUS ERAS of the Church's history, various aspects of God's character have been stressed, such as his holiness, his righteousness, and his sovereignty. Today the focus of attention is on his love. No doubt many could echo Robert Browning's statement in *Paracelsus*, "God! Thou art love! I build my faith on that." To be sure there is truth in this assertion. The problem is that current speculations about the love of God tend to be more cultural than biblical. So it is important to understand something about God's love as Holy Scripture defines it by both precept and illustration.

It is often said that the love of God is unconditional. There is biblical support for this. One of the most familiar verses in the Bible declares that "God so loved the world that he gave his only begotten Son." The Apostle Paul spoke of it this way: "God commendeth his love toward us, in that, while we were yet sinners, Christ died for us." Manifestly, the redemptive love of God is not dependent on the sinner's response and continues to be available today in the gospel.

God's love is also unconditional as far as our relationship to him is concerned. An illustration of this can be seen in the story of the Prodigal Son. Even though he wasted his substance in riotous living he was received back when he returned

to the father's house. If God's love for us were dependent on our behavior as Christians, it would be more like our love than his. Every Christian should be grateful for the constancy of his heavenly Father's love.

In such a context, it may be asked whether this is all that can be said about the love of God: that it is unconditional, accepting, and forgiving. Scripture discloses another characteristic. God's love is also purposeful. At this point the biblical description of God's love runs counter to the modern conceptions that seem to say, "He is always ready to forgive," and stop there. But the Word of God in Hebrews 12 specifies that whom the Lord loves, he chastens, and that he scourges every son whom he receives.

The remarkable thing about this statement is its assertion that the chastening of God is an evidence of his love. In addition, one of the visible signs of our redemption and relationship to God is that we are chastened by him. Moreover, this chastening is not necessarily because of disobedience. When Jesus was asked the question, "Master, who did sin, this man, or his parents, that he was born blind?" his reply was, "Neither hath this man sinned, nor his parents: but that the works of God should be made manifest in him" (John 9:2, 3). Similarly, the chastening ministry of God is not only because of misdeeds but also for the purposeful development of the individual.

There are illustrations of this in Scripture. One of the most remarkable is that of God's only begotten Son. Apparently, this same principle applied to him. The writer of Hebrews declares that the Lord Jesus, even though he was a son, learned obedience by the things he suffered, and being made complete by this testing became the author of salvation to as many as obey him. And so in the unique experience of Christ himself, especially when on the cross he cried out, "My God, my God, why hast thou forsaken me?" there was a chastening experience which, in some mysterious way, provided a completeness for him.

Another instance is the experience of Job, a man who was careful to do the will of God and yet suffered severely. Because of God's love for him, Job learned much through his experience. He could say, "Now mine eye seeth thee. Wherefore, I abhor myself, and repent in dust and ashes." In spite of his righteousness, which was commendatory, the chastening experience revealed the necessity of a new perspective on his relationship to God.

Early in his life Joseph learned of the purposes of God for him. Yet for years he was despised by his brothers, cast into prison, and generally misunderstood. Still he continued faithful until the time when God honored him, so that he could say to his brothers, "You meant it for evil, but God meant it for good."

David was described as a man after God's own heart; but from the time when he was anointed to be king, he was beset with difficulty. There were persecutions before he took office and troubles and heartaches after he was crowned. Yet throughout his life the chastening love of God resulted in blessing.

The Apostle Paul certainly experienced God's love. In retrospect he could say, "We glory in tribulations also, knowing that tribulation worketh patience; and patience, experience; and experience, hope. And hope maketh not ashamed; because the love of God is shed abroad in our hearts by the Holy Ghost which is given unto us" (Rom. 5:3-5). In reflecting on his own life he remarked, " . . .will I rather glory in my infirmities, that the power of Christ may rest upon me" (2 Cor. 12:9).

Consider also the great heroes of the faith listed in Hebrews 11. It was said of them, "And these all having obtained a good report through faith, received not the promise." During the long centuries of the church's history there have been those who experienced terrible suffering, often culminating in the loss of their lives. They died in faith, believing that the inscrutable purposes of God would be worked out even though for them there was never the completeness of blessing that characterized the lives of others such as Job, Joseph, David, and the Apostle Paul.

There is another dimension of God's love illustrated in the account of the rich young ruler. Scripture says that the Lord Jesus, looking on him, loved him and then said, "Sell [what] thou hast, and give to the poor, and thou shalt have treasure in heaven: and come and follow me" (Matt. 19:21).

It is this that C. S. Lewis had in mind when he penned in *The Problem of Pain:* "You asked for a loving God: you have one. The great spirit you so lightly invoked, the 'lord of terrible aspect,' is present: not a senile benevolence that drowsily wishes you to be happy in your own way, not the cold philanthropy of a conscientious magistrate, nor the care of a host who feels responsible for the comfort of his guests, but the consuming fire Himself, the Love that made the worlds, persistent as the artist's love for his work and despotic as a man's love for a dog, provident and venerable as a father's love for a child, jealous, inexorable, exacting as love between the sexes."

Thus, God's love is not only unconditional and purposeful, but also incredibly and totally demanding. It requires of us all that we are and have.

Such love has goals for us. The writer of Hebrews makes clear that the loving chastening of the Lord is "that we might be partakers of his holiness." As we understand this, it should also be one of the central aspects of our love for him. Jonathan Edwards, in his *Treatise Concerning Religious Affections,* said, "A true love to God must begin with a delight in His holiness and not with a delight in any other attribute, for no other attribute is truly lovely without this."

Another objective for those exercised by God's chastening love is to produce the peaceable fruits of righteousness. As God's love is made manifest in our hearts and lives, our understanding of it cannot simply be abstract but must be expressed in obedient action. This is what our Lord Jesus Christ had in mind when he said, "If you love me, keep my commandments." He himself confessed that he loved the Father and the

Father loved him, and so he did always those things that pleased his heavenly Father. In light of this, we should not be deluded by the antinomianism of our age, for the authentic response to God's love is unconditional obedience. This is why our Savior, when he established the claims of discipleship, specified these conditions: "If any man come to me and hate not his father, and mother, and wife, and children, and brethren, and sisters, yea, and his own life also, he cannot be my disciple" (Luke 14:26). Until there is this kind of response to God's love, our discipleship is inadequate and incomplete.

An understanding of God's love not only affects our relationship to him but also the age in which we live. This is both negative and positive. It is essential to recognize the antithesis of which the Apostle John speaks: "Love not the world, neither the things that are in the world. If any man love the world, the love of the Father is not in him. For all that is in the world, the lust of the flesh, and the lust of the eyes, and the pride of life, is not of the Father, but is of the world" (1 John 2:15, 16).

We should learn now rather than later by costly experience that love for God and love for the world cannot exist together. There operates in the Christian's life a principle of displacement, so to speak; for it is not possible at one and the same time to have love for God and love for the corruptness, the lustfulness, the pride, and the self-seeking that are characteristic of this age. The two are mutually incompatible. If we really understand God's love and the response he expects of us, we know he will tolerate no other claim on our affections. He must be sovereign if we are to enjoy a meaningful relationship with him.

On the positive side, the First Epistle of John specifies that love for God finds its tangible expression in love for one another. Yet this is because God first loved us. St. Augustine had this in mind in his work *De gratia Christi* when he said, "In order that we might receive that love whereby we should love, we were ourselves loved while as yet we had it not." It is the provision of God's love that enables us to love another.

Miss Helen Keller was one of the outstanding figures in our American history. She was born in 1880 and at the age of nineteen months suffered an illness that resulted in blindness and the loss of speech. When she was six years old, her parents implored Dr. Alexander Graham Bell to see if there was something he could do to help their daughter. At his suggestion Anne Sullivan, who herself had been at the Perkins School for the Blind in Boston because of poor eyesight, came to take charge of the little girl who was then quite ungovernable. Because Helen resisted any kind of discipline, Miss Sullivan had to be very harsh with her. In one dramatic encounter at the dinner table, Helen pounded on the table and created a scene. Miss Sullivan, despite the objections of Helen's father, dragged the child outside and forced her to come to terms with her teacher. She and Helen were by the pump in the yard. As the little girl reached out her hand and felt the water, she succeeded for the first time in forming the word "water." When the father took her back, Miss Sullivan felt that despite what had happened at the pump she had lost the child. Yet in one of the most poignant incidents of the entire experience, the child returned to Miss Sullivan, reached up to touch her face, identified it as that of her teacher, and very gently kissed her on the cheek.

Did Miss Sullivan love the child? There was no question about it. Thankfully, Helen Keller came to realize that her teacher's stern discipline was an evidence of love so that she might develop a capability to learn. And as all the world knows, this gifted woman became one of the most celebrated personalities of our time. Yet this was because her teacher was the kind of person who had a love that was akin to the love of God—a love that was not permissive but highly directive, that when necessary was harsh and stern, but always for the ultimate good of the child.

The world today has a distorted view of the love of God. Yet there can be an understanding of his love in Christ as the gospel is preached. By means of this declaration Christians can enable the world, with its confusion, its self-seeking, and its perversions, to come to an understanding of God's love. This understanding can be reinforced through the demonstration of the poignancy and depth of Christian commitment —a commitment akin to the Apostle Paul's for his own people when he said, "I could wish that myself were accursed from Christ for my brethren, my kinsmen according to the flesh." This can be the product of our understanding of God's unconditional but purposeful and exacting love. Today's generation longs for something that is genuine. Those who have known God's love can enable the world to understand its authentic reality.

# 1970
## *The Judgment of Words*

ONE OF the strange paradoxes of our times is this: never before has there been a greater torrent of words both written and spoken to clamor for our attention, while at the same time few of us can imagine or remember a time when there was a more profound sense of mistrust and alienation. Not everyone expected things to turn out this way. Years ago, Robert Hutchins voiced the hope that as men communicated more effectively, they would come to understand one another better and live in greater harmony. The opposite appears to be the case. If anything, the rise in literacy and increased educational opportunity have tended to accentuate an attitude of arrogance on the one hand or a sense of threat on the other.

Furthermore, the misuse of media for the purpose of manipulation has created what we now call the credibility gap. Whether there be distrust of the pronouncements of a head of government or of the statements of employees calling in "sick," everyone is supposed to know "the rules of the game." The *double entendre* applies today to more than suggestive jokes. Yet despite all this, a vague sense of the wrongness of this situation still persists.

I am not one who believes that the leaders of today are necessarily less honest than those of a previous era. It is simply

FOR CHRIST
AND
HIS KINGDOM
1927

that now the possibility of denying that something had been said has virtually vanished. Instant replay is difficult to refute. In fact, for the first time in history man is approaching in a limited way a manner of life in which he can be held accountable for what he has said. Yet the issue of integrity is sufficiently significant to move some to invoke a situation ethic to justify the contradiction between what had been said and what is the truth.

Despite the atmosphere of distrust and the popularity of the thesis that verbal communication is passing away, we still have a daily newspaper circulation of over sixty million. Many thousands of new book titles are published each year in addition to thousands more of new editions. The United States and its possessions have over seven thousand radio stations and hundreds more television stations. Obviously, verbalization is not yet passé as a means of communication. In fact, Steven Kelman has suggested in his book *Push Comes to Shove* that some of the most radical elements in our culture are the most committed to the printed word.

Consider also that the law of contract remains as an indispensable part of our economic and social life. Giving our word, despite the abuse of trust in this day and age, is still an expectation. Furthermore, meaningful human relations continue to depend on "talking things out."

Within the Christian community the importance of words can scarcely be overestimated. Repeatedly Scripture describes God's communication with man in the simple phrase "and God said." It is striking to note that God did not choose primarily to convey his revelation subjectively or interpersonally or through events and encounters but used Scripture to verbalize his message to man. Furthermore, it is the proclamation of the good news that fulfills the great commission, and man's response involves a confession of Jesus Christ as Savior and Lord. Even in the eternity to come there will be verbal exclamations of praise.

Despite this there are those who would insist that actions

must replace words even in the area of Christian witness. In the volume *Rethinking Missions,* the editor, William Ernest Hocking, declared that service in the name of Christ is evangelism in the best sense of the term. As if to support this a professor at one of our eastern colleges told me on one occasion that Jesus never talked about what he believed but only demonstrated his convictions by doing good. My reply was that this was not the record of the Gospels. Hence, in an effort to avoid the stigma of the classification of our confession as "just words" we must not make action the exclusive vehicle of our witness. Surely if anyone were capable of doing this, it would have been our Savior. That he chose to speak as well as act should be instructive to us.

Let it be granted that words as well as actions are God-given means of communication and that God has chosen to speak as well as act in disclosing his truth. Let it also be granted that one of man's distinguishing characteristics is speech. Then it is reasonable to assume that others will judge us by what we say as well as by what we do. Yet this immediately raises questions in the minds of the thoughtful individual. He considers the difficulty of communication between cultures. To depreciate this problem would be to reduce in significance God's action at the Tower of Babel. Even more puzzling is the fact that among those who have the same language there is persistent misunderstanding. What parent is there who has not repeatedly said to his children, "But I told you," or "How many times do I have to tell you?" Nor is the problem limited to the parent-child relationship. We are all too familiar with the problem of why the same statement is so differently interpreted by individuals who simultaneously happen to hear it.

The issue here, however, is not how human beings judge the speech of another, but rather how God uses the judgment of words in his dealings with man. I suggest that this can be considered in two aspects. First of all, the words of God judge us. What sensitive and informed Christian has not been struck with the judgmental quality of Holy Scripture as the Spirit of

God has used the Word of God to speak to a particular circumstance or action? I believe this is so in view of the statement: "Wherewithal shall a young man cleanse his way? by taking heed thereto according to thy word" (Psa. 119:9). Furthermore, the affirmation that "the entrance of thy words giveth light; it giveth understanding unto the simple" (Psa. 119:130) suggests that the Word of God judges in the sense of establishing value or significance.

Biblical truth can have a very searching and pervasive penetration of the individual. Consider the statement of the writer of Hebrews that the Word of God is living and active, piercing even to the dividing asunder of soul and spirit and joints and marrow and is a discerner of the thoughts and intents of the heart. God's statements to us in Holy Scripture, therefore, both provide conviction for wrongdoing and also validation for that which is consistent with the will of God.

Not only do the words of God in Scripture judge the individual, but the words of the individual are subject to God's judgment. Our Savior said, "By thy words thou shalt be justified and by thy words thou shalt be condemned." He further indicated that for every idle word men speak, they will give an account of themselves to God.

The key to all of this lies in our Savior's statement that it is out of the abundance of the heart that the mouth speaks. The opening verses of Romans 10 make clear that the term "heart" is used in Scripture in more than a narrowly specific sense. It can be a term to identify the total personality of the individual.

It is the "abundance" of the essential nature of the individual that is really the source of speech. But what is this abundance? The term is that which also is found in Mark 8:8 where it is used to describe the surplus food that was left over after the multitudes had been fed. When this meaning is applied to the inner life of the individual, it seems clear that speech is the natural outflowing of the real attitude of the individual.

Illustrations of this abound. Those who are deeply concerned about something tend constantly to talk about it, unless there is a deliberate effort to turn the conversation into another channel or there is some inhibiting factor that restrains free expression. So it is not difficult to see why it would be entirely appropriate for God to judge man for that which is the manifestation of the attitude of his heart. Scripture observes that where our treasure is, there will our heart be also. So if our concerns are antithetical to the will of God, our speech will reflect this.

There is a qualitative element to God's judgment of our words. This is mentioned in our Savior's statement that men will give an account to God for every idle word they have said. The term "idle" implies what is unfruitful or barren. The imagery is of faith without works. We conclude then that where there is barren or unfruitful speech, this is the necessary product of a life in this spiritual condition. The Apostle James spoke of this in the third chapter of his epistle when he deplored the contradiction of speech but suggested that this reflects the contradiction in man's inner state.

The obvious way to deal with the problem of the judgment of words, therefore, is to consider first of all the state of our inward condition. The Apostle James says that where there is bitter envying and strife in the heart there is the expected product of every evil work. When we recognize also that our Savior declared the subsequent actions of an individual are really the reflections of his heart attitude, it is not difficult to see that speech and action are interrelated.

One of the most tragic accounts in all of Scripture is that in which our Savior is confronted by those who called him "Lord, Lord," and yet were fated to have him respond by saying he never knew them. In a very real sense their ejaculation was an idle word, for it was devoid of real commitment. And so we will be subjected to the judgment of our words not only as to the correctness of what we say but as to the integrity of meaning behind these words. When our speech reflects a straightforwardness of heart, we can confidently expect the blessing of God; when it does not, we can be sure of his judgment.

It is here that the ministry of the blessed Holy Spirit is essential. One of the most significant acts of God in history was Pentecost. This not only enabled individuals to hear in their own language the Word of God but also made possible an authentic articulation between man and God. The Apostle Paul observed that no one can call Jesus "Lord," in the true sense of the term, apart from the Spirit of God. Moreover, it is the bestowal of God's gift of the Holy Spirit that enables us to speak in a way which is well pleasing to him. This in turn is the natural expression of the fruit of the Spirit in the inner man, and it is also the product of the informing ministry of the Holy Spirit in making the truth of the Word of God real to us.

We ought to speak out of the abundance of our hearts in such a manner as to bring honor and praise to Jesus Christ because of our obedience to the Word of God and our openness to the Holy Spirit. The authenticity of our witness ought not only merit the blessing of God but also the approbation of men. It is this kind of witness that can commend the Christian message to those who have judged other pronouncements and found them wanting. It merits the consideration of the perceptive but searching individuals of our time who need to come to terms with him who said, "And ye shall know the truth, and the truth shall make you free." They too are subject to his declaration, "By thy words thou shalt be justified and by thy words thou shalt be condemned." Let the abundance of our hearts prompt us to confess our authentic commitment to Christ as Savior and Lord. In so doing we will fulfill his command to be witnesses unto him and merit his "well done" in that day when our words as well as our deeds will be judged of God.

# 1971
## *Not Many Wise*

THE SCRIPTURAL statement that not many wise are chosen of God may appear puzzling at first. Man made in the image of God has intelligence superior to any other of his creatures, and it would seem evident that man should necessarily have opportunity to use this capability for God's glory. Furthermore, wisdom and knowledge are surely desirable, for the Proverbs repeatedly stress the value of obtaining them. Beyond this is the commandment to love the Lord our God with all of our minds, an obligation that is required of every believer.

The problem essentially is the way in which man uses his capability of knowing. The opening chapters of the Bible describe his temptation and fall. It is the nature of the temptation and man's response to it that is of crucial significance. Satan's proposal was that Adam and Eve could gain a knowledge of good and evil characteristic of deity. Thus, the temptation basically was to attract man to the status of equality with God. Despite man's fall and subsequent estrangement from God, he has never ceased to aspire to this status and strives continually to gain equality with God. Since God will never share his glory with another, man remains as a challenger who can never be successful. Nevertheless, he is compulsively motivated to try. Indeed, recent scientific discoveries have prompted some to declare that at last man is in a position to be master of his fate—a divine prerogative.

This assessment of man's achievement highlights the biblical teaching that the primary scene of the struggle for man's allegiance is in his mind. Since it is true that "as a man thinketh in his heart, so is he," the convictions he reaches are critical to his whole manner of life. Those who are the best informed constantly are tempted to consider themselves competent to render judgment about things ultimate as well as things immediate as far as their value or significance are concerned.

Cain provides an example of this out of man's earliest history. The offering he brought to the Lord was that which he determined would be acceptable. When God rejected his offering and hence his judgment, he was angry. Presumably even the Lord himself should not have questioned Cain's evaluation. In his self-will, Cain acted as if his perception was equal to God's.

The results of this kind of speculation are stated categorically by the Apostle Paul in the first chapter of his Epistle to the Romans: "They did not like to retain God in their knowledge." In the same epistle he affirms that the carnal mind is not subject to the law of God, neither indeed can be. These statements are consistent with our Savior's observation that it is out of the heart of man that evil thoughts come and these in turn produce evil actions. The record of man's history provides ample validation of this predisposition of man to think and act in a manner calculated to challenge God's Word and ultimately his sovereign rule over man.

Nor is this limited to those who by circumstance have been denied the opportunity for an encounter with the Word of God. In the Old Testament, Solomon stands as a tragic figure who clearly understood God's commandments and was supernaturally gifted with wisdom, and yet deliberately chose to disobey God. In the New Testament the intelligentsia of the day were the Pharisees, Sadducees, and scribes. Their intensive knowledge of Scripture unfortunately was not sufficient to overcome their ambition to advance themselves. This search for personal fulfillment caused them to contrive various clever devices in order to circumvent the clear teachings of Scripture and thus indulge their own desires.

Even the Apostle Peter, after he had committed himself to be a disciple of Christ, fell prey to this tendency. After the Lord announced his forthcoming death, Peter began to rebuke Jesus with the clear implication that he knew better than his Master. The Savior's response is symbolic of the divine judgment on such presumption and is consistent with the prophetic word in the second Psalm as to God's forthright rejection of those who challenge his sovereignty.

The Christian intellectual then needs to realize the persistence of this human tendency to seek equality with God and to recognize that even within the believing community this ambition is not necessarily absent. Moreover, it is evident that the possibility of such an attitude is so great that God uses particular care in selecting from the ranks of the intellectuals those few whom he is able to use.

The basis for God's selection of them rests to a considerable degree on their positive response to the commandment to love the Lord their God with all their minds. In his gracious provision for mankind God has disclosed himself in ways that are of particular significance to those gifted with keenness of mind. The redeemed scientist as well as the aesthetically sensitive believer can rejoice in God's disclosure of himself in nature. Christians who are perceptive in self-knowledge and knowledgeable in interpersonal relationships recognize that God created man in his own image and that even though this image is marred, it still remains extraordinarily wonderful. These insights, however, can be complete only as they are informed by the Word of God.

It is the task of the Christian scholar to study intensively the text and meaning of Holy Scripture in order to relate the Word of God in a coherent way to the whole spectrum of learning.

Indeed, it is the recognition of the need for the integration of faith and learning that has provided one of the most inspiring challenges to the Christian intellectual. Together with the Psalmist, the Christian scholar can exclaim that the precepts of the Lord are his delight.

Yet the motivation for all of this transcends simply a love of learning as such. Perhaps it could be stated this way: One of the marks of love for another is a desire to know the other person better and to be interested in those things that are of significance to him. The Christian scholar who has committed himself to love Jesus Christ finds a delight in those things that relate to his Lord and Master. As the Savior reverenced the Word of God, so does the Christian scholar. Christ's unconditional obedience to his Father should have its counterpart in the redeemed intellectual. Our Savior's obvious awareness of people as well as nature is a pattern for the Christian scholar to follow. So commitment to Christ ought to be our basic motivation. From this can come the involvement of the mind in the things that are Christ's because of his creative and redemptive acts and because of his manner of life in his earthly ministry.

To the believing scholar, there is the promise that obedience to the divine commandments will result in a greater awareness of God himself. In John 14 Christ specified that a positive response to his commandments would bring about a greater degree of intimacy with the Father, himself, and the Holy Spirit. In a remarkable way, then, the relatively few intellectuals who are chosen are privileged indeed, for to them is given the holy privilege of experiencing this divine disclosure. Yet as obedient disciples, they must continue to recognize and accept their subordination under Christ's lordship.

The voluntary acceptance of this subordinate role is of utmost importance. In the Apostle Paul's discourse in the closing verses of 1 Corinthians 1 and the opening section of chapter 2 he establishes at least two reasons why not many wise are chosen. The first of these is that no flesh should glory in God's presence. Yet the attempt to do so seems characteristic of the academic community. This persistent challenge to the sovereignty of God inevitably results in a forfeiture of one's eligibility for being chosen of God as his intellectual. And so the divine-human relationship must be clearly distinguished from one of equality and seen as the subordination of the Christian intellectual to the sovereignty of God. Any capabilities possessed by the intellectual and any opportunities for their utilization are wholly of God. Once this is understood, then those few that are chosen do not presume that they have any right to glory in God's presence but instead accord all of the glory to him.

The other reason is not Godward but manward. The Apostle indicated that he came to the Corinthian church in weakness and fear, not parading his enormous intellectual capabilities. The reason for this was that their faith should not stand in the wisdom of men but in the power of God.

Some years ago a young woman professed faith in Jesus Christ. Later she repudiated this. When inquiry was made as to the reason, it was discovered that actually she had placed her faith in a brilliant Christian intellectual rather than in the Lord himself. When she was no longer able to maintain an association with this gifted Christian, her faith collapsed. Centuries before, the Apostle Paul had clearly foreseen this danger. So it is the difficult and necessary task of a Christian scholar to ensure that his relationship to others does not result in their faith being located in his wisdom instead of in the power of God. It may well be necessary for him regularly to affirm that he knows in part and understands in part, and that God is the source of whatever wisdom he has.

To avoid the presumption of glorying in the presence of God or the temptation to assemble a personal following rather than leading people to Christ, the Christian scholar who will be part of the chosen minority must have a manner of life characterized by rigorous self-discipline. Such discipline begins first in the mind and is described by the Apostle Paul in 2 Corinthians 10:5. He recognized that human imaginations will persistently exalt themselves against God. The task of the Christian intellectual is to cast these down and lead captive every thought to the obedience of Christ.

Our Savior, as the living Word, is a striking example of that which should characterize our own mental self-discipline. He could affirm, "Not my will but thine be done." The Christian is obliged to recognize the inherent tendency for his thought life to rise in challenge to the sovereignty of God. As he seeks to cast down these imaginations and lead captive every thought to the obedience of Christ, he will apply the normative standards of the Word of God. Simply a generalization that one will be subordinate to the lordship of Christ is not enough. As the Word of God was primary in the life of Christ, so it must be in the life of the Christian scholar. This means that there will necessarily be a tension between the point of view adopted by the scholar and that of his unbelieving contemporaries in the intellectual world. Yet one cannot be God's chosen one unless he deliberately resolves that for him every thought is to be led captive to the obedience of Christ.

At this point the matter of reputation becomes crucial for some. Understandably they desire acceptance in the intellectual world. Here the example of Christ becomes particularly instructive. In Paul's Epistle to the Philippians there is the exhortation to let this mind be in us which was also in Christ Jesus. What follows is a clear indication that reputation or status cannot supersede obedience. Our Savior willingly laid aside his glory to be obedient, even though it meant death on the cross. Similarly, the cross must influence the manner of life of the Christian intellectual if he is to be among the few whom God can use. Indeed, his response to the commandment in Philippians must involve his willingness to sacrifice recognition and acceptance among his peers, if necessary, in order to be identified with God and his Word.

This is not a simple matter and it is costly. Yet it was Christ himself who established the demanding conditions of discipleship and specified that unless one was willing to pay the price, he could not be his disciple. The Christian scholar is obliged to face squarely the claims of Christ in the area of the mind so that his commitment to him as Lord in this important dimension of life may be realistic and complete.

Yet it would be an incomplete portrayal if discipline were perceived as the only significant factor in God's calling of the wise. In Philippians 4 the Christian scholar in particular is exhorted to think on the things that are true, honest, just, pure, lovely, and of good report. This suggests that there is not only discipline but delight in being God's chosen ones in Christian scholarship. Here is the place in which virtue and praise can be the proper recompense of the informed Christian. Indeed, the inspiration in thinking God's thoughts after him provides sufficient reward to the disciplined, humble, and instructed Christian.

God seeks for men and women of splendid intellectual endowments and academic prowess whom he can use. These are they who will not seek to challenge God's glory nor divert the allegiance of believers from God to themselves. As followers of Jesus Christ, they seek to let his mind be in them. By making this their aim they can have the privilege of fulfilling the will of God even as in an absolute and complete sense our Savior did in his earthly ministry. In so doing they will furnish to the world, to the community of God's people, and—most important—to their Lord and Master a practical exemplification of true wisdom.

# 1972
## *The Crisis of Allegiance*

THE WORD of God is filled with incidents that in their application are strikingly contemporary. One of these is recorded in Luke 18 in the account of the rich young ruler. In many respects he is representative of modern man. He was young. The usage of this term in Scripture implies that he was between twenty-four and forty years of age. To some that may not seem young, but from the perspective of the Bible it is. And while many in our country are not yet that old, such an age group represents about 40 million Americans.

He is also described as a ruler. This did not necessarily mean a person who held a political office, but might well have been someone who was appointed to an ecclesiastical position. Conceivably this young man was a member of the Sanhedrin, and if so, was held in respect and honor by those who were of the religious community. He was also affluent, for Scripture says that he was very rich. In today's terms he was probably a millionaire.

Few of us would consider ourselves to be in any of these categories. Yet compared to most of the world's population, we are richly endowed with vitality, affluence, and prestige. Despite this, we often have a feeling of incompleteness. We may have achieved status. We may have attained prosperity.

We may have enjoyed the best of health and the opportunity for a meaningful life. Nevertheless, a vague uneasiness persists that these things are not all that give life significance, and we seek—sometimes desperately—for someone who can answer the basic questions of human existence.

Those who were involved in the "Jesus Revolution" dramatically and eloquently showed that there are values other than being a ruler, or being very rich, or even being young. Others of our contemporaries have tragically illustrated the fact that it is possible to have all of these advantages and still find life to be without hope or meaning.

Out of a similar sense of need this young man came to our Lord Jesus Christ. The major issue in the encounter with our Savior was not wealth, although that is sometimes assumed to be the case. It was rather a crisis of allegiance involving the exercise of sovereignty. So it was not just that the young man had possessions. It was rather their influence over his decision that was the issue.

This important question is considered in the Gospel of Luke in both a logical and a chronological sequence. It should be borne in mind that material things are not inherently evil but have been given to us by God for our enjoyment and blessing. Furthermore, the material possessions cited in the passages we are about to consider are representative of whatever resources we may have, whether money, property, ability, or opportunity. In other words, they are anything that is committed to us for our stewardship.

Luke 12 includes the well-known story of the rich fool. This man used knowledge gained by observation to arrive at his conclusions. Probably he had seen his friends and neighbors pull down their barns and build greater ones so they could have material wealth for many years. And on the basis of this observation he determined to do the same thing.

At first glance this would seem to have been prudent and worthy of commendation. Yet the Lord said to him, "Thou fool, this night thy soul shall be required of thee: then whose shall those things be which thou hast provided?'' The rebuke was fully justified because of the inference the man drew from his projected actions. He thought that by simply controlling his possessions through placing them in storage for future usage he was able to determine his future. The Lord's response was to point out how incomplete his observations were. While some did indeed live on for many years and enjoy their wealth, others did not and neither would he. Ultimately, his life was not controlled by himself at all but by God's sovereign will. Because of his preoccupation with the material things of life, the rich fool failed to perceive this basic truth.

Another instance is found in Luke 16—the well-known story of the rich man and Lazarus. In Hades the rich man cried out to Father Abraham and urged that he send Lazarus to go and speak to his five brothers. Abraham's reply was: "They have Moses and the prophets: let them hear them." In desperation the rich man argued that if someone came to them from the dead, they would listen. Abraham's response to this is of compelling significance. He pointed out that if the five brothers would not heed Moses and the prophets, neither would they respond if one came to them from the dead. In other words, even as had been true of the rich man himself, the five brothers had become so preoccupied with what they thought were essential matters and had so governed their lives by these considerations that even the clear teachings of Scripture were inconsequential. Apparently no matter how forcefully the Word of God spoke to the issues of life and death, it was not effective to overcome the predilection of these people to seek to control their own destiny by handling for themselves the resources they had.

Furthermore, this preoccupation had become so overpowering that even if someone returned to them from the dead with a warning, it would not be heeded. As an illustration of this, consider the reaction of people generally to the raising of Jesus Christ from the dead. He came back to confront a culture that was caught up in its own immediate concerns. To be sure, there were hundreds that responded; there were scores of thousands who did not.

In Luke 18, as well as in Matthew 19 and Mark 10, there is the account of the rich young ruler. This provides an illustration of communication through personal encounter. We have seen that the perspective of the rich fool was inadequate since he failed to take into account those who did not live a long time. In his overly optimistic framework of reference these were not significant. We have also observed that with respect to biblical truth, the rich man's brothers permitted their preoccupation with their resources to make them so insensitive that they would ultimately ignore even the miracle of a resurrection from the dead. By contrast, in this instance the rich young ruler on his own initiative sought an encounter with a personality whom he obviously considered capable of telling him what he wanted to know.

It is instructive to us to see how our Lord dealt with this young man as he knelt before him, calling him Good Master and indicating his desire to obtain eternal life. Rather than addressing himself immediately to the request, our Savior responded by questioning the title the young man gave to him: "Why do you call me good?" We may infer that the meaning being conveyed to the young man was, "Why do you call me perfectly good?" Then Jesus in effect said to the young man, "Think for a moment—there is only One who is perfectly good and that is God." By such means the Savior sought to draw the young man's attention to the real significance of his seeking out Jesus to ask him his question. Did he really perceive the One he called "Good Master" as actually God manifest in the flesh?

Christ then proceeded to deal with the young man's question by referring him to the commandments, the law of God. When the young man responded by indicating his obedience to these and asked what he yet lacked, the Lord dramatically disclosed himself as the Divine Lawgiver, the only one who could at that point presume to set forth conditions by which the young man would have "treasure in heaven." Furthermore, this was not to result simply from obedience to what the Lord commanded, but it also involved a commitment to the person of Christ himself: "Follow me." Yet all of this was to be subsequent to his selling everything that he had and giving the proceeds to the poor.

Clearly, what was at issue was not the material possessions of the young man, but rather the way in which he perceived values. On the authority of Christ's statement, if he gave his fortune away he would not be poor but rich; for he was promised treasure in heaven. Yet this was governed by whether or not he was prepared to acknowledge Jesus Christ as God and therefore a Sovereign to be worshiped by being obeyed.

This is the decision that confronts all of us, whether we have an abundance of material goods or not. The fact is that God has committed to our care not only things material, but also our relationships, abilities, and opportunities. All of these are part of our resources, and it is to these that the Savior refers when he inquires whether we perceive him as Lord—as God manifest in the flesh. If so, are we prepared to obey him on his terms? Let us not deceive ourselves about this. It is costly, for it involves our possessions, our loved ones, and even life itself.

On one occasion my wife and I attended a service of worship in a church in the East. The minister announced that one of the congregation had a statement to make. A man came forward and shared with us that his wife had just died after a long illness. With conviction he spoke about what a difference it had made in their lives when they came to know Jesus Christ as Savior and Lord about a year before. Prior to that time they had been unable to face the possibility of being separated by death, but after receiving Christ they realized that her illness and their destiny were in his gracious hands whether in life or in death. Then he said, "I believe she is more alive today than she has ever been before," and encouraged us not to be sad but to rejoice, because Jesus as her Lord had taken her to himself. All of us were deeply moved. This was beautiful. Here was a person one year old in Jesus Christ who had been asked in a sense to pay the price of giving up that which was dearest to him, but who had come to a perception of what all of this meant. He could rejoice through his tears. This illustrates both the cost and the rewards of accepting the lordship of Christ.

When our Savior spoke to the rich young man, I believe he asked him to relinquish his right to everything that was significant to him. He was rich. The Lord Jesus said, "Sell all that you have and give to the poor." He was young. The Lord Jesus summoned him to a discipleship that involved the taking up of the cross. He was a ruler. The command was, "Follow me." In response the young man went away sorrowful.

Yet we may not be justified in concluding that he once for all rejected the loving claims of Christ on his life. F. Crowsley Morgan, the son of G. Campbell Morgan, in preaching on this particular subject emphasized that the Bible does not specify that the young man went away and never returned to Jesus Christ. The issue was left unresolved. Scripture is silent as to what happened. It is at least possible that he ultimately did come back to the Savior and gave him his unconditional allegiance.

We may have the riches of ability and opportunity and we may perceive Jesus Christ as good and therefore God. But whether or not we respond to his sovereign claims by in effect selling all that we have and taking up our cross and following him is a decision that is up to each individual. *This is our crisis of allegiance.*

# 1973
## *The Validation*
## *of Discipleship*

DISCIPLESHIP is generally associated with religion. Every faith has those who are classified as disciples. Usually this term is understood to mean a follower or adherent. Yet its definition is more comprehensive than this. A disciple is also a learner, one who has placed himself under the tutelage of a master. As far as Christianity is concerned, the primary relationship of master and disciple is between the Lord Jesus and his followers. Within the church, however, he has gifted some to be teachers so that the people of God can be instructed in the truth of his revelation. Indeed, this is the specific mission of Christian education, with the students being, in the best sense of the term, disciples. Yet their learning is not simply the development of understanding but includes as well the encouragement to commitment to Christ as Lord and Master.

Discipleship should not be confused with sonship or the relationship the Christian has as a child of God. On occasion it is suggested that a Christian's primary function is to enjoy the security and blessing of belonging to the family of God. While we quite properly may rejoice in this vital relationship, there is a distinction between this and the status of discipleship which one assumes voluntarily. Yet we should not overlook the fact that Scripture speaks of obedient children and teaches that when we are born again we become new creatures, and as such gain a new cognitive ability—an ability to know the things of God through the teaching ministry of the Holy Spirit.

So there are these two major elements in the term *disciple* —learning and obedience. Because we are free as those who have been redeemed by the sacrifice of Christ, we have the privilege of discipleship under the lordship of Christ. Furthermore, it is he who establishes the terms of our discipleship and defines what the validation of that discipleship is.

In Luke 14 our Savior enunciated the conditions that must be met by those who would be his disciples. First of all, unless we perceive all other relationships—even the highest and the holiest, such as marriage, parenthood, or those of children to father and mother—as subordinate to Christ we cannot be his disciples. It may be difficult for us at first to accept this condition; yet we must recognize that our Lord, if he is to be sovereign, cannot tolerate any allegiance that challenges or supersedes what he requires of us as his disciples.

He also asks that there be a constant reaffirmation of our commitment. Sometimes we perceive discipleship to be a one-time declaration, an allegiance pledged at a point in time in the past. Our Savior recognized the human tendency toward forgetfulness and preoccupation, and so specified that we are to take up the cross *daily* and follow him or we cannot be his disciples. This means that there is to be a regular renewal of the unconditional giving of ourselves unto him.

Then he cites the condition of our counting the cost. To explain this he used the illustrations of building a tower or of going out to battle. Thoughtfully and realistically we must calculate what it means to give up all we have; otherwise, we cannot be his disciples.

So these conditions—the precedence of our relationship to Christ, the daily renewal of our commitment to him, and the renunciation of all that we are and have to his sovereign will —must be accepted before we are really justified in calling

———— *Dr. Armerding with Dr. Richard Linyard and Mrs. Ruth Graham, trustees of Wheaton College.*

ourselves his disciples. Otherwise, we may be children of the heavenly Father, but we are not disciples of the Lord of glory.

The life of the Apostle Peter illustrates the fact that our Savior will hold us accountable for what we say. Almost glibly, Peter said, "Lord, we have left all and followed thee." Very soon after that he was subjected to a testing which disclosed just how superficial his affirmation had been. Then on the occasion of his restoration the Lord not only assigned him the ministry of feeding his lambs and tending his sheep, but also told him there would come a time in his life when he would be led where he did not want to go and would have his hands stretched forth, signifying the death that Peter was to die.

This illustration is of importance in understanding the demands of discipleship, particularly in our success-oriented culture. Too often the impression is given that when one becomes a disciple of Jesus Christ he is guaranteed affluence, or status, or solutions to his problems. To be sure, this can happen; but this is only part of the picture. For example, Peter enjoyed the privilege of welcoming the Gentiles into the body of Christ. As best we know, he also suffered death by crucifixion. It is well to recognize, therefore, that there are blessings and privileges in discipleship; but this does not justify the unrealistic optimism that assumes that problems and difficulties will no longer be present in the life of the Christian.

This was recognized by the Apostle Paul. In his testimony he acknowledged that although he had been born an Israelite, was privileged to be a Pharisee, and had a commendable record of righteous living, yet he was obliged to conclude: "I count all things but loss for the excellency of the knowledge of Christ Jesus my Lord." Nor was this merely rhetoric. He suffered scourging, stoning, imprisonment, and shipwreck for the cause of Christ. On the other hand he could also say: "I know how to be abased, and I know how to abound. . . .I can do all things through Christ which strengtheneth me."

Both Peter and Paul learned that when Jesus Christ summoned them to be his disciples he expected them to understand the conditions of that discipleship and voluntarily to make a commitment that was perceptive, realistic, and irrevocable.

Once we have understood and accepted the conditions of discipleship, then we need also to recognize the criteria by which such discipleship is validated. These are found in the Gospel of John. The first of these is in chapter 8, verse 31, where the Lord Jesus says: "If ye continue in my word, then are ye my disciples indeed; and ye shall know the truth and the truth shall make you free." One knows that he is a disciple when his whole manner of life is governed by the Word of Christ.

In the lives of Christians there is inevitably a conflict between the Word of God and the word of man, a struggle known by many firsthand. Constantly the question arises: "Yes, hath God said?" Regularly the temptation is to advance our own opinions so we can "be as gods, knowing good and evil." As disciples, however, we must validate our discipleship by determining to continue in the Word of God. The glorious truth is that the product of obedience is disclosure. The more we obey the Word of the Lord, the more we will know that truth that sets us free.

The second of the criteria is in John 13:35: "By this shall all men know that ye are my disciples, if ye have love one to another." Sometimes this is perceived as loving the lovely. It is doubtful that our Lord had this in mind because it is not much of a test to love a charming, attractive Christian. Whether we care to admit it or not, there are unloving and unlovely Christians. Yet our obedience to the command to love them may result in mutual blessing.

Some years ago a fellow Christian made it his business to record my public statements at an annual convention, then followed it up with a report in which he indicated what he considered to be wrong with what I said. Finally I asked him if he would go to dinner with me. As we talked together I told him that while I recognized that we disagreed profoundly on some very important aspects of ecclesiology, I accepted him as a Christian brother and loved him in Jesus Christ. His reaction was heartwarming. He felt free to share with me some concerns in his life because now he had accepted me as a fellow believer, even though we differed on important points of church practice. His subsequent reports, while critical, were also more charitable. What caused the change? God by his grace made it possible to love someone who naturally was not very attractive. The result was a drawing together of two believers in Jesus Christ who recognized their honest differences but still respected and loved one another.

The third criterion is in John 15:8 where the Savior says that if we bear much fruit then we are his disciples. In his illustration of the vine and the branches the Lord makes clear that the fruit will necessarily be characteristic of the vine, and this is because the branch "abides" in the vine.

Some years ago I became acquainted with a very well known preacher. On occasion I listened to his associates. It was interesting to note that they pronounced words and used phrases that were the same as the minister under whom they were working. The reason was obvious. They were so intimately associated with him, respected him so highly, and had accepted so much of his manner of life that they were unconsciously reflecting the characteristics of his speech. In a far more comprehensive way the Christian who is vitally related to the Lord Jesus, learning from him and adhering to what he says, comes progressively in time to be like him. The result will be that our manner of life will remind others of Jesus Christ.

There are some Christians, however, who believe that discipleship is something that can be taken up for a time, and then put aside. Such believers lack the strength and stability produced by obedience. The Lord Jesus Christ illustrated this in his famous story of a man who built a house on a rock and another who built on the sand. Our Savior explained that the one was akin to the person who heard his sayings and did them, and the other like the person who heard his sayings and did not do them. We may speculate why on occasion an ostensibly strong Christian has crumbled under the testing and proving of life. There may very well have been a lack of obedience, a rejection of known truth that eventually was manifested in the stress of circumstance.

Dr. Dennis L. Meadows and a group of associates have published a provocative book called *The Limits to Growth*. One prediction is that at the rate at which the resources of the world are being used and the rate at which its population is growing, we have only until the end of the twenty-first century before the world will have exhausted its resources. The solution is to limit growth, but there is little hope that this is possible. If the prediction is valid, we may soon enter a period of testing and proving that will ascertain what kind of foundation Christians have for their lives. Then will be disclosed whether our discipleship was as unequivocal and unconditional as our Savior said it should be. The prospect could fill us with a sense of dismay were it not for the reassuring words of our Lord and Master to those who would follow him: "Come unto me, all ye that labour and are heavy laden, and I will give you rest. Take my yoke upon you and learn of me; for I am meek and lowly in heart: and ye shall find rest unto your souls" (Matt. 11:28).

Grace E. McFarlane, special instructor at the Conservatory of Music, Wheaton College.

# 1974
## *For the Glory of God*

IN MEDIEVAL TIMES a Latin phrase in common usage was, "To the glory of God." Reflecting this conviction, Ignatius Loyola formed the Society of Jesus and chose as its motto, "For the Greater Glory of God." The composer Johann Sebastian Bach made a habit of signing his works, "Sole Deo Gloria." In this same spirit Billy Graham is noted for repeatedly giving praise and glory to the Lord for whatever impact his ministry has had, being convinced that if he did not, his ministry would soon fall into disrepute.

Unfortunately, this concept is largely ignored in our culture. Instead, the major emphasis is on self-fulfillment. Rather than living for the glory of God, modern man seeks for what will satisfy his desires. This is not to imply that self-satisfaction is illegitimate, but in God's economy it ought to be subordinate.

In 1972 the Carnegie Commission on Higher Education issued a report entitled, "Reform on Campus." The authors suggested that whereas one hundred years ago it was necessary to modernize higher education because of the advent of industry and technology, now it was necessary to humanize education in order to make it more responsive to personal needs. This is understandable, but there is a growing disagreement as to the scope of human needs. Furthermore, there is confusion about moral, ethical, and spiritual values and how these relate to self-fulfillment.

The *Chronicle for Higher Education* in 1974 published a survey by a recognized public opinion poll agency. In 1969 young people from the ages of sixteen to twenty-five were surveyed. Then, four years later, the survey was repeated—asking the same questions. The results were startling. In 1969, 45 percent of those polled thought leading a clean, moral life was appropriate. By 1973 the percentage had dropped to 34.

In response to a question about premarital sex, 34 percent of those surveyed in 1969 were opposed. By 1973, this had declined to 22 percent. In 1969, 77 percent agreed that extramarital relations were not appropriate. By last year this had become 66 percent. In light of these statistics it is perhaps significant that in 1969 38 percent felt that religious values were important in their lives. Four years later the percentage was 28.

This survey suggests that our culture is less and less inclined to live in accordance with divine prescriptions. Instead, each individual is expected to make his own moral and ethical choices.

The priority of self-fulfillment is also becoming evident among evangelicals. Recently a letter from the North Africa Mission, authored by Dr. Francis Steele, made the point that whereas evangelical churches are growing in numbers and in affluence, today the missionary enterprise suffers from both an inadequate number of candidates and insufficient financial support.

To counterbalance this, appeals to Christian service are often made on the basis of need. A film is shown or statistics are cited in such a way as to arouse the emotions and produce a response. Yet later, when the immensity of the need is viewed in light of the relative paucity of resources, it is easy to become discouraged. Excitement has been replaced by harsh reality, and the possibility of a romantic experience seems remote.

Another effort to generate a personal response is the possibility of limited service. I am grateful for the opportunity many persons are given to spend a short term abroad, but I am troubled by the thought that this may be utilized to retain the option to withdraw, rather than to make an irrevocable commitment that could be altered only under the sovereign direction of our Lord Jesus Christ. We may be in danger of abandoning the conviction that living so as to glorify God is to be our primary motivation rather than responding to human need or selecting revocable options that are exciting at the moment.

Once we have determined to serve under the direction of our Sovereign Lord we need to understand what the glory of God actually is. Someone has said, "As light and heat are to the sun, so glory is to God." There is a sense in which the glory of God is revealed to all men. The 19th Psalm and the first chapter of the Epistle to the Romans suggest that we may see something of God's glory if we will look at the creation. The manifestations we see in nature are indications of God's power and glory, of his majesty and greatness.

While all men have the capability of recognizing God's disclosure of himself in nature, our perception of God's glory becomes more acute as a result of our becoming Christians. George Wade Robinson has expressed it this way:

> *Heaven above is softer blue,*
> *Earth around is sweeter green!*
> *Something lives in every hue*
> *Christless eyes have never seen.*

This is illustrated by a story about two people who were walking together in a large city. A coin dropped on the sidewalk. One of the two heard it fall and immediately began looking for it. At the same time a bird was singing and the other person at once heard this melodious sound. The ear of the one was attuned to the clang of a coin falling on the pavement, but the ear of the other was sensitive to the song of a bird. A richer and fuller perception of God's glory comes from the sensitivity that God gives to us in redemption.

There is also a special sense in which the Lord's servants may observe something of God's glory on those occasions when they become aware of him through an unusual experience. In the account of Exodus 33, Moses had the sublime opportunity of seeing the divine glory in his personal encounter with God. Isaiah, in the 6th chapter of his prophecy, was deeply moved as he saw the Lord, "high and lifted up."

Often when we think of the glory of God we relate it to activity, remembering the Scripture, "Whether therefore you eat, or drink, or whatsoever ye do, do all to the glory of God" (1 Cor. 10:31). But there is a prerequisite to action and that is contemplation. The Apostle Paul says, in 2 Corinthians 3:18, "But we all, with [unveiled] face, beholding as in a glass the glory of the Lord, are changed into the same image from glory to glory, even as by the Spirit of the Lord."

Contemplation or meditation is seldom practiced because of the frantic schedules we all have. You may believe that once you have completed a particular task life will become more tranquil. This is improbable. If you become meaningfully involved in life, you will have increasing demands on your time and energies. Yet you can also develop a greater capacity to manage these pressures if you do so intelligently. One way is to take time to meditate on the Word of God and by the Holy Spirit think about the person and work of the Lord Jesus.

As was true of the Apostle Paul, there will increasingly be the realization that there is nothing in ourselves of worth that can be brought to God. But as there is the contemplation of the Lord of glory, there comes the recognition of his all-sufficiency in fitting us for his service. Then, when the question comes, "Whom shall I send and who will go for us?" it will be possible to say, "Here am I, cleansed, fitted, given a vision of greatness. Send me."

The Lord Jesus said that fruitbearing was not only an evidence of discipleship but it was also that which glorified God.

We know that fruit is the visible evidence of the essential nature of a plant. So our Lord Jesus was teaching that what is produced by the abiding Christian is characteristic of the vine itself. This means that as you and I contemplate our Lord Jesus Christ and allow his life to characterize us, the product will be expressed in Christian action. It cannot be the reverse. There is no fruit apart from the vitality of the vine. So it is with you and me. We first must have newness of life. Then as the life of Jesus becomes more and more revealed in us, we will bear much fruit.

In a sense we are incarnations of the very life of Christ. On this basis we are able to fulfill the Scripture which says that we should do all to the glory of God. Often such activity is perceived very negatively and is described only as a matter of deprivation or denial. To be sure, discipline is part of discipleship but there is also a special sense in which there is joy. For example, John the Baptist said of our Lord Jesus Christ, "He must increase, but I must decrease." This was not a statement of futility. Rather, as John gave his life wholly to glorify Jesus Christ, this produced an ineffable sense of satisfaction and fulfillment.

On one occasion a man was at a social affair with his wife. She was enjoying herself immensely, talking and laughing. It was interesting to observe the face of the man. He was beaming. The fact that his beloved was fully enjoying herself gave him a tremendous sense of fulfillment. This illustrates what happens in our lives as we live for the glory of God. We find fulfillment in seeing God glorified, his name magnified, and his cause advanced. Indeed, it requires discipline, it takes time, it will involve sacrifice, and it presumes an irrevocable commitment. Yet, when we seek to do all to the glory of God, by his marvelous provision we find a fulfillment that this age persistently seeks and just as consistently fails to find.

So it is with confidence in a faithful and loving heavenly Father that I commend this principle of life to you: Seek by his grace to do all for the glory of God.

81

# 1975
## *The Understanding Heart*

FOR MANY OF US the term *heart* refers to that part of us that is primarily emotional, that yearns or desires, that loves. The biblical usage, however, is more extensive. Scripture defines the heart as that which characterizes us as persons, particularly as God sees us. When Samuel undertook the task of anointing a successor to Saul, he looked at the sons of Jesse and was impressed with them. To save him from a superficial judgment, the Lord reminded him that man looks on the outward appearance but God looks on the heart. For that reason he preferred David. In other words, he sees us as we really are.

The Apostle Paul delineated the various aspects of the term *heart* in Romans 10. In the first verse he says, "My heart's desire and prayer to God for Israel is, that they might be saved." This was an expression of deep emotional feeling for his fellow countrymen. In the sixth verse the Apostle's comment is, "Say not in thine heart, Who shall ascend into heaven (that is, to bring Christ down from above)." This was an indication that the heart is where reflective thought takes place. Then in the tenth verse Paul declares, "For with the heart man believeth unto righteousness." So the understanding heart is characterized by feeling, thinking, and deciding.

That being so, what does Scripture mean when it says of

our Lord's disciples, "They considered not the miracle of the loaves for their heart was hardened"? The condition of their hearts indicated they were part of sinful humanity, for in the fall of man his heart was radically altered. The affections that should have been directed toward God were turned toward self. Instead of being able to pray in sincerity, "Thy will be done on earth as it is in heaven," mankind has parodied our Savior's prayer in the Garden by saying in effect, "My will, not Thine, be done." And as far as his intellect is concerned, man has decided to think for himself. Indeed, it was this possibility that the Enemy presented to Adam and Eve when he said, "Ye shall be as gods knowing good and evil." In other words, they would determine for themselves what was good and what was evil.

Pharaoh's reaction to Moses and Aaron illustrates this. There is repeated evidence of the hardness of Pharaoh's heart. In spite of the strong warnings of Moses and Aaron and the great plagues that came on Egypt, Pharaoh was determined to have his own way. His emotional outbursts continually manifested this. His will was inflexible in spite of all the things that had happened to him and to his country. His mind was unable to relate the phenomena of the plagues to the hand of God.

The same may be said of the Pharisees. In spite of their reputation as defenders of the Word of God, they dedicated themselves to the task of circumventing its clear teachings. They deluded themselves into believing they could simultaneously affirm and deny the commandments of God. Even within the early church, Ananias and Sapphira, after seeing the supernatural power of God at work, decided that by clever misrepresentation they could pretend to give sacrificially and thus attain the status of others who had sold their possessions and laid the proceeds at the apostles' feet. How could they have attempted such an absurd thing? It was simply because their hearts were hardened. An inordinate desire for status gripped them; so they cleverly schemed how they could deceive the apostles and then deliberately decided on a course of action. The severity of the judgment on them makes clear that God held them accountable for the hardness of their hearts even as he did Pharaoh and the Pharisees.

There is a limitation caused by hardness of heart that affects cognitive ability. Illustrations of this are found in the account in Mark 6 of the disciples' reaction to Jesus' walking on the water and in Mark 8 in their inference about the Lord's warnings against the leaven of the Pharisees.

Consider the experiences through which the disciples had passed. They had participated in the feeding of the five thousand and of the four thousand. On both occasions the Lord confronted them with the issue of how such large groups of people were to be fed. Then he took what resources they had and performed a miracle before their very eyes. Quite probably they were skeptical as they watched the Lord take such a small amount of food, offer thanks, and then give it to them for distribution to the people. Yet as they kept returning there was always more, until all had eaten. Even more remarkable, there was a substantial surplus collected afterward. They could not fail to get the point: Their Lord possessed supernatural power.

Yet when the Lord walked on the water and then calmed the storm, the disciples were amazed, taken by surprise that he could do these things. Furthermore, when he told them to beware of the leaven of the Pharisees, they could only infer he was hinting about their forgetting to take bread with them. Apparently the disciples found it impossible to relate the two miracles of feeding the multitudes to his ability to walk on the water or to meet their need for bread.

There is no intimation that there was anything wrong with the disciples' ability to observe. As active participants they knew from their own experience what had actually happened. Despite this, they failed to grasp the meaning the miracles were to convey about the person of Christ.

This is graphically illustrated by the Apostle Peter in the

account of his response to our Lord's statements as found in Matthew 16. When Jesus asked his disciples, "Who do you say that I am?" Peter answered, "Thou art the Christ, the Son of the living God." Jesus explained that flesh and blood had not revealed this to him, but instead it had been disclosed by the heavenly Father. Yet when Jesus then told his disciples he was going to be taken by wicked hands and crucified, Peter took issue with him. This was despite the fact that Peter had just been the recipient of an extraordinary revelation from God, enabling him to call Jesus the Messiah, the Son of the living God. Peter was unable to relate his affirmation about the person of Christ to an acceptance of our Lord's authoritative declaration about what was to happen.

By way of contrast, consider Abraham when God ordered him to take his son Isaac and offer him as a sacrifice. Anyone who has been a father could understand to some degree what must have passed through Abraham's mind. But the issue was more than a father's being asked to kill his beloved son, incredible as this was. Earlier, God had told him that in Isaac a divine covenant would be established. So it was not only that he was being directed to do away with his own offspring, but also that this would contradict the covenant promises God had made to him. Yet Abraham obeyed.

To understand this, it is necessary to consider the circumstances of Isaac's birth. Both Abraham and Sarah were past the time for bringing forth children, and so the birth of Isaac was a miracle. Abraham must have concluded, therefore, that since God had performed one miracle so that he and his wife became parents, God could perform a second miracle and raise his son from the dead. It would be no more difficult for him to do that than to have brought Isaac into the world in the first place.

Abraham's response was evidence that he had an understanding heart. He looked beyond the paradox of God's apparently contradictory statements and trusted the faithfulness and power of God. That is why he was able to subordinate his natural emotions and respond immediately to what he was asked to do.

The Apostle Paul manifested this same ability to understand. In chapter 5 of the Epistle to the Romans he made a statement that to many would seem absurd: "We glory in tribulations." Then he specified that this was based on an understanding that tribulation works patience, and patience experience, and experience hope, and hope makes not ashamed, because the love of God is shed abroad in our hearts by the Holy Spirit who is given to us.

This is the perspective of the understanding heart. It is not achieved except by the gracious ministry of the Holy Spirit. In chapter 2 of 1 Corinthians Paul emphasizes that eye has not seen, nor has ear heard, nor have entered into the heart of man the things that God has prepared for those that love him. In other words, he had learned that an understanding heart was the product of more than observation or historical report or human speculation. It is this: "God hath revealed them unto us by His Spirit, for the Spirit searcheth all things, yea, the deep things of God" (1 Cor. 2:10).

One incident in the life of the Apostle particularly illustrates this. Three times he asked the Lord to take away his thorn in the flesh. When the Lord's response was that his grace was sufficient for Paul, there was no more remonstrance or pleading. Because he had an understanding heart, Paul could glory in his weakness and affliction.

Many Christian college graduates do extraordinarily well in college. They accumulate a considerable body of knowledge and demonstrate that they can think logically and perceptively. But it is still possible for them to be graduated with a hardened heart, having all the information the disciples had, as well as the experience of observing supernatural things happen, and still determine not to accept the Word of God as normative or to acknowledge Jesus Christ as Lord. Instead, self-advancement and self-aggrandizement can be primary, with the assumption that life can be lived apart from the Lord because of a misguided trust in personal ability and knowledge.

We must recognize that Christian education is complete only when the result is an understanding heart that can affirm with the Apostle Paul, "I have learned in whatsoever state I am, therewith to be content. I know both how to be abased and I know how to abound, everywhere and in all things I am instructed both to be full and to be hungry, both to abound and to suffer need." This is because the mind is informed by the authoritative statements of Holy Scripture; the emotions are moved to love the Lord with all the heart, soul, mind, and strength; and the will does acknowledge Jesus Christ as both Savior and Lord.

May God grant that Christian higher education will continue to develop an understanding heart in its graduates.

# 1976
## *Unto You It Is Given to Know*

IN THE PARABLE of the sower our Lord described the ways in which the Word of God is received. Nowhere in the parable is there any question about the integrity or the quality of the Word. Instead, the issue is how those who heard the Word responded to it. Nor is there any doubt about the meaning of the parable. In response to the disciples' request, Jesus interpreted what he had said. It is his explanation, therefore, that enables us to understand this parable.

I recognize that many believe the parable refers to four different groups of people. This is entirely possible. I suggest, however, that the parable can also be seen as describing the reactions of an individual at various times in his life. The experiences of the Apostle Peter provide an illustration of this.

Consider the first category of the seed by the wayside. When the Word is declared, it is not understood. Then Satan snatches it away to prevent it from ever being received into the heart and life of the individual. Probably we have all at one time or another experienced this. Right after we have heard an eloquent and forceful presentation of the Word of God, some chance remark or some incident immediately diverts our attention. The reason for this, however, is more than external. Inwardly, the Word was not understood. More often than not this is because there is a predisposition in the life of the individual not to receive it.

These elements may be seen in Peter's confession of Jesus as the Christ and then his subsequent attempt to rebuke him (Matt. 16:13 ff.). When the Lord asked the disciples, "Who say ye that I am?" it was Peter who declared that he was the Christ. But then, after Jesus told them he was to be taken by wicked men and be crucified, Peter began to rebuke him and actually contradicted his Lord.

What made Peter react this way? Despite his confession with its recognition of the unique character of our Lord Jesus Christ, he felt personally threatened when the Lord talked about suffering and dying. After all, Peter had become a disciple of Jesus. If his Master was to suffer and die, what then would become of him? Thus he was not willing to accept this word from his Lord. Immediately Satan took advantage of this. We know this is so because as soon as the Lord heard Peter's rebuke, he turned and said to him, "Get thee behind me, Satan: thou art an offense unto me: for thou savourest not the things that be of God, but those that be of men."

The second category is the seed on stony ground. Our Lord explained that this represents those who accept the Word with joy and gladness. Then when tribulation or difficulty comes, they no longer maintain the commitment they have made. Some of us know this also by personal experience. Following a powerful emotional appeal we have responded. Then shortly afterward, when the implications of what we have done become apparent, we repudiate our stand. Why? I believe it is because our decision was one-dimensional. Our response to the preaching of the Word, however, ought to be multi-dimensional. Certainly emotion has its proper place. Wesley could say that his heart was strangely warmed at the chapel on Aldersgate Street. But unless the mind grasps the meaning of Scripture and the will resolutely commits us to its truth, our response remains one-dimensional and thus inadequate.

Peter also had this kind of experience (Matt. 26:33-35). After Jesus told his disciples that they would be offended because of him, Peter replied that even though all the others would respond that way, he would not. When the Lord emphasized that even Peter would deny him, Peter insisted that even if he were to die with Jesus, he would never deny him. Yet as soon as a maid identified him as a companion of Jesus, Peter pretended that he did not know what she was talking about. When others made the same point, he became the more emphatic in his denial.

What went wrong? It seems to me that Peter was sincere in his enthusiastic pledge to be faithful to the Lord even if it meant giving up his life for him. But then when he saw Jesus captured and sensed the hostility of the group and their evil intentions, he immediately recognized that his identification with Jesus was personally threatening. At that point his one-dimensional commitment caused him to be offended and to deny the Lord Jesus three times.

The seed in the third category fell where there were thorns and briers, and thus bore no fruit. The Lord explained that this represents those who hear the Word, go forth and become so preoccupied with the concerns, the riches, and the pleasures of this life that the Word cannot be fruitful. Here again this may have been our experience. I have been in a church service listening to the preaching of the Word, when I began to think of the responsibilities of tomorrow, my financial obligations, or something that had to do with my personal well-being. Soon I was not listening at all because of my preoccupation with these other things. Yet how much more serious it is when one's manner of life is so overburdened with cares, so preoccupied with financial concerns, and so absorbed with self-indulgence that Scripture increasingly has no place in his life.

From Peter's life we have an illustration of this kind of preoccupation. In Acts 10 there is the account of Peter falling into a trance while at prayer and seeing a sheet lowered from heaven. On it were creatures that, as a Jew, he was forbidden to eat. Then he heard a voice saying, "Rise, Peter, kill and eat." In reply he objected that he had never eaten anything that was common or unclean. Then the voice spoke, "What God hath cleansed, that call not thou common." Three times the experience was repeated for emphasis.

Then the messengers came with Cornelius's invitation and Peter was told by the Holy Spirit to go to the Gentiles—people with whom he would not normally associate. As a result God used him to introduce the gospel to them. When the council at Jerusalem took up this matter, Peter explained to the leaders of the church what had happened. Hearing his testimony, the leaders accepted the fact that God had directed Peter in his actions.

In spite of this, an incident occurred at Antioch in which the Apostle Paul was involved (Gal. 2:11). Peter had been freely associating with the Gentiles until Jews sent by James came to him. At that point he dissociated himself from the Gentiles. In light of his experience with the household of Cornelius, how could he do this? I suspect it was because at that moment he became deeply concerned about his status with his own people. What would they say when they found out he had been associating with Gentiles? So he withdrew from his fellow believers until the Apostle Paul, in the presence of all of them, rebuked him for his inconsistency. In other words, Paul urged him to be obedient to the revelation he had received on the housetop and not permit circumstances or the expediency of the moment or concern for his own well-being to turn him aside from that which he very well knew, and which had been so dramatically mediated to him.

In the fourth category are they that receive the Word, understand it, and bring forth fruit. What is this fruit about which our Lord was speaking? His statements in John 15 help us to understand this. He said that if we abide in him and his Word abides in us, we bear much fruit. To me, abiding is to be conformed to the Lord's will in obedience. Furthermore, in John 8

Jesus said that those who are his disciples indeed are those who keep his commandments. So the disciple is the one who bears fruit by making his Lord's Word the governing principle of his life.

Peter also came to illustrate this, as can be seen from the testimony of his two epistles. Instead of resisting his Lord's word, he now accepted it and did so with full understanding and realistic commitment. Recognizing that he would lose his life for Jesus' sake, he did not object or question. As he matured in Christ, he was bringing forth fruit because he was prepared to do what the sovereign Lord asked of him.

I believe that accepting the Lord Jesus as personal Savior not only makes us part of the body of Christ, but also furnishes us with both the capacity and the opportunity to understand God's truth. Notice that the Lord explained the parable only to his disciples. He quoted from Isaiah 6:9, 10 to indicate why the others who heard the parable would not have the explanation given to them. Their hearts had become insensitive, and their ears dull of hearing. This was because they were not open to God's truth due to their persistent rejection of it.

This is consistent with what other Scriptures teach. In Romans the Apostle Paul says the people of the world did not like to retain God in their knowledge so God gave them up to a reprobate mind, to do those things that were not appropriate. On the other hand the Lord explained the parable to his disciples because they had committed themselves to him.

"Unto you it is given to know" is a phrase applicable to those who, by confession of faith in Christ, have come into the family of the redeemed and, by commitment to his lordship, are the disciples of Jesus Christ. Yet this privileged status carries with it an important responsibility. When our Savior finished explaining this parable, he reminded his disciples that no one who lights a candle puts it under a bed or under a bushel basket. Instead, he puts it on the lampstand, so that it may give light. Then he warned them to take heed how they hear because to those who have, more shall be given; but from those who have not, even that which they seem to have will be taken away.

Through the ministry of faithful servants of God we have had opportunity to understand Holy Scripture. We have had pointed out to us the evidences of God's revelation in nature and in man. In truth it can be said of us as it was of the disciples, "Blessed are your eyes, for they see: and your ears, for they hear" (Matt. 13:16). Yet we must remember that these privileges and advantages carry with them a corresponding responsibility. As in redemption we responded to his truth, so we should continue to respond in obedience to the Word that we hear, to the light that we see. For unto *us* it has been given to know.

May it increasingly be said of us that we have grown in knowledge because we have grown in obedience. Let us remember our Lord Jesus' statement in John 8, "If ye continue in my word, then are ye my disciples indeed; and ye shall know the truth, and the truth shall make you free."

# 1977
## *His Mind in You*

EARLY in this century there was a best seller, written by Charles H. Sheldon, entitled *In His Steps*. It had as its thesis, "What would Jesus do?" Mr. Sheldon believed that if we could follow the practices of Jesus, our lives would tend more and more to reflect his character and purpose in life.

Those of us who are evangelicals have been reluctant to accept this proposition because of its abuse by some earnest but misguided people. They have assumed that if they could imitate our Lord Jesus Christ and in the process become good enough, God would accept them.

Yet we cannot dismiss the example of Christ as irrelevant. The reason is the emphasis it receives in Holy Scripture. The Apostle Peter in the second chapter of his first epistle tells us that the Lord Jesus left an example that we should follow his steps. Indeed, this is the biblical reference that Mr. Sheldon used as the title for his book. Also, Philippians 2:5-11 emphasizes that we should have the mind of Christ, that is, that the same attitude and perspective that characterized our Lord Jesus Christ should be true of us as well. In effect, we are to follow his example by the way in which we order our minds.

The mind matters. We know that the mind matters not only because its cultivation broadens our perspective, but also because Scripture teaches that there is an integral relationship between what we think and what we do. The writer of Proverbs 23:7, speaking about mankind, commented "as he thinketh in his heart, so is he." Our Lord Jesus Christ in Matthew 15:19 said, "Out of the heart proceed evil thoughts," and then listed the actions that result from these thoughts.

Having the mind of Christ will safeguard us from such thoughts. It will also enable us to think constructively and to act in accordance with biblically oriented principles, even as Jesus did.

One of the major characteristics of our Savior's viewpoint was that, although he was in the form of God, he did not think that equality with God was something that he should seek to retain. The New International Version puts it this way: "Who, being in very nature God, did not consider equality with God something to be grasped" (Phil. 2:6). If we are to have the mind of Christ we need to ask ourselves what this meant in the experience of our Lord.

I think it applied in two dimensions; first, with respect to status, and second, to relationship. When the Scripture says that he did not consider his status something to be grasped, we recognize that he was lowering himself and taking a subordinate position to that which rightfully was his as God the Son. The ancient creeds affirm that each of the persons of the Godhead is equal in power and glory. But our Lord Jesus Christ did not cling to this which was rightfully his, but deliberately set it aside.

There is also the matter of relationship. You recall how the early verses of Genesis describe the act of creation. "Let us make man in our image, after our likeness." There was a concert of purpose and action on the part of the three persons of the Godhead. When our Lord Jesus Christ voluntarily limited himself and took a subordinate position, he did not cease to be God the Son. But his relationship was different. As a result he acknowledged the sovereignty of God the Father over him, so that he could say, "I do always those things that please my father."

In light of these considerations how should we respond if we are to have the mind of Christ? First, we need to recognize something that is common to mankind and even present in the Christian community as well. This is the inherent aspiration to seek to elevate ourselves to the position of God. We still respond to the temptation, first presented in the Garden of Eden, that we should be as gods knowing good and evil.

I find that in my own life there are regularly challenges to the statements of the Word of God that are there for me to obey. In effect, I believe that perhaps my idea is better or possibly I have a plan of action that is superior to that which God has ordained in his Holy Word. In doing this I am seeking the status which was sought by Adam and Eve—to decide for myself what is good and what is evil. From my experience I have found that this issue must be addressed squarely.

Consider a biblical illustration. In the 16th chapter of Matthew, the Apostle Peter confessed that Jesus was the Christ, the Son of the Living God. Jesus' response was to call him blessed and to indicate this confession was a revelation from God the Father to him. Then the Lord told his disciples he was going to suffer and die. At that, the same apostle who called him the Christ now said to him, "Not so, Lord."

Too often you and I confront a clear, unambiguous statement of Holy Scripture and in effect say, "Not so, Lord." Yet if we are to have the mind of Christ, this viewpoint must be dismissed from our thinking. We must recognize that when God speaks we are not to presume that we have a status of equality with him. Instead, having the mind of Christ will enable us voluntarily to acknowledge our subordination to his will and purpose.

As far as relationship is concerned, we should keep in mind the conditions of discipleship that our Savior established and how these relate to his own action. These conditions are set forth in Luke 14:26: "If any man come to me, and hate not his father, and mother, and wife, and children, and brethren, and sisters, yea, and his own life also, he cannot be my disciple." We know that Jesus did not mean that we should ignore these relationships. This would be in violation of other portions of Scripture. But what he was saying was that to be his disciple there has to be a new view of these relationships. Just as our Lord Jesus Christ, having had an integral relationship with the Father and with the Holy Spirit in eternity past, assumed a subordinate position, thus altering what had been, so he says to us that if we are to have his mind, we must recognize that these natural, normal, and God-ordained relationships must be perceived in a new way.

I assure you that this will not be easy. For example, many young couples want to do what their parents have suggested. Those who are married will want to do what their spouses would like them to do. And children's interests and needs modify what parents think they should do. The conflict is between these normal and necessary concerns and that which God has established as our primary allegiance, namely to himself.

Furthermore, Scripture says that the Lord Jesus not only did not cling to status or relationship but also made himself nothing. I cannot adequately comprehend this. How One who is infinite in power and glory as one of the three persons of the Godhead could deliberately make himself nothing and cross this enormous span of status and relationship to the point of the most basic subordination, is beyond the scope of my understanding. But at least I can get from this what is expected of me if I have the mind of Christ.

The Apostle Paul in using the word "servant" in this passage selected a term that means bondservant or slave. In other words, awesome as it may seem to us, our Lord Jesus Christ took upon himself the form of a slave. How could he do this? I believe it was because of what went before. Not grasping for that which was rightfully his and not endeavoring to maintain his relationships unchanged, he then was able to take this subordinate position and become a servant. All of this was preparation for what followed. Having become a bondservant, he was then prepared to face the ultimate test of obedience—the cross.

As we do not cling to status but assume a subordinate position and as we are willing to put other relationships into a peripheral place so that the primacy of our relationship with the Lord Jesus might be central, then there comes the challenge of obedience. Here we often differ from our Savior. We make our obedience conditional. We say that if he will do certain things, then we will become his bondservants. Or, our service is spasmodic. We will be obedient in response to a particular opportunity on a special day and under favorable circumstances.

You no doubt have heard of a current marriage ceremony which says that the couple are to be faithful one to another as long as they both shall *love*. In other words, the commitment is conditional. As long as each manifests love to the other, the relationship will be maintained. But if one no longer demonstrates love, this justifies breaking the relationship.

Perhaps this is the way we have approached our service for Jesus Christ by saying to him that as long as he recompenses us by bestowing his blessings and benefits, we will serve him. But when our Savior was put to the test and upon the cross cried out, "My God, why have you forsaken me?" he did not abandon his role as Savior. Scripture says he endured the cross, despising the shame.

There may well be occasions in your experience and mine when there will not be an immediate recompense. From the eleventh chapter of Hebrews we know that not all Christians have received in this life the benefits and blessings that God has bestowed upon others. Instead, they died in faith, not having received the promise. In this or other ways God will permit you to be tested if you have indeed determined that you will have the mind of Christ in setting aside status, modifying relationships, being willing to take a position of a bond-servant, and making your obedience unconditional.

Do you remember the scene at the seashore when the Lord Jesus had prepared a meal for the disciples? After they had eaten, he turned to Peter and asked him three times whether he loved him. After Peter responded, our Lord told him that there would come a time when people would take him where he did not want to go. Thereafter, the Apostle Peter knew very well that his expression of love and his willingness to be a bondservant of Jesus Christ would have its ultimate test. As you know, the tradition is that he was crucified upside down and in this way showed his commitment to his Savior.

The Scripture we are considering, however, has still another emphasis. Having spoken about the self-limiting action of our Lord Jesus Christ it says, "God also hath highly exalted him, and given him a name which is above every other name: that at the name of Jesus every knee should bow, of things in heaven and things in earth, and things under the earth; and that every tongue should confess that Jesus Christ is Lord, to the glory of God the Father."

Is this something that should also be in our perspective? I believe it is. Many people are concerned about a career, wondering what they will be doing in life. Others have an idea of what they will do, but this may be modified in the future, depending upon circumstances. In either case some may be tempted to take matters into their own hands to ensure that their careers are in place and not left to chance. This could involve special arrangements or even manipulation to be certain that they will get what they want.

Let me suggest another point of view. I believe that if we are to have the mind of Christ, we will need to recognize that there must be a fullness of time, so to speak, before a ministry is opened to us. We may have difficulty accepting this at this point because it may seem too uncertain. Yet I am convinced we should wait until God's time is right and then he will show us the way.

Consider Moses. At the age of forty he thought the time had come for him to become the leader of his people. So he took matters into his own hands. When he saw a terrible wrong being inflicted upon one of his countrymen, he killed the Egyptian. The result was that he had to flee the country and for forty years live on the backside of the desert. Superficially we might say these were wasted years. On the contrary, they were years of preparation for Moses and also the exact interval of time that was necessary until the conditions were precisely right for the deliverance of God's people. When Moses attempted to act on his own, neither was he ready nor were the conditions right. But when God called him out of the wilderness, the sovereign purposes of the Lord were fulfilled in accordance with the divine timetable. I am certain that in looking back Moses recognized it was better to wait until God was ready.

Or consider Joseph. He had an extraordinary experience in having these dreams from God about how his father and mother and brothers would all bow down to him. But then what happened to him? There was one setback after another. He was captured by his brethren and sold as a slave, taken into Egypt, betrayed, put into prison and left to languish there forgotten. Perhaps into his mind might have come the thought that God had mocked him and told him things that obviously never came true. After all, he was not even with his father and mother or his brethren but in a foreign land and in jail at that, with no hope of ever getting out. But he learned that when he was ready and the conditions were right, God would fulfil his promises.

So, do not be afraid to trust God. If you have the mind of Christ, you can wait for God's timing, meanwhile doing faithfully that to which God has called you. When you are ready and when the conditions are ready, I can assure you out of my own experience, the door will open. God will open it. And because you are ready and the conditions are right, you can be confident of his blessing. He will exalt you in due time.

There is one other aspect of this perspective. Scripture says that the Lord Jesus was highly exalted. The Word of God also says that we shall reign with him. For those who are concerned that at this time they will not get that which others might receive, be encouraged. There is coming a day in which his provision and his reward will be given to those who love and serve him, not because we are worthy but because we are related to him.

So let us have his mind in us and be prepared and ready for his will to be worked out through us so that in his own good time we might have his "well done" bestowed upon us.

# 1978
## The Challenge
## of Success

IF I were to ask you what your definition of success is, your reply might vary but probably would include such things as status, power, influence, or wealth. These characteristics of success may have prompted this observation about success: it is the degree to which other people envy you.

This may explain why many people believe that success provides for personal fulfillment. Successful people are envied because it is assumed they have achieved their goals in life and thus have experienced maximum satisfaction.

Some notable illustrations would suggest that this is not necessarily the case. Rather than success improving the quality of life or providing personal fulfillment, it has for some resulted in disillusionment and despair.

Twenty years ago Robert Young was nationally known as a successful financier and railroad executive. He had made millions of dollars and had experienced the exhilaration of challenging his corporate opponents and winning the battle. Thus his career was perceived as immensely successful. Yet when his railroad empire began to be in difficulty, Young was unable to find in his past success the resource that he needed. One morning after breakfast in his palatial Florida home he walked into the recreation room, took a shotgun, and ended his life.

Two years ago a private airplane was en route to Houston, Texas, with a famous passenger who required emergency medical treatment. Before the plane landed in Houston, however, the man died. He was Howard Hughes, one of the richest men in the world. Earlier in his life he had won a number of trophies because of his ability as an aviator. He also produced several films that were box office triumphs. The business he inherited from his father was extraordinarily prosperous. Yet after his death it was disclosed that for twenty years Howard Hughes had been heavily dependent upon drugs and lived in a chronic state of euphoria. This may explain why he was virtually a recluse during this time and why some have questioned the validity of the agreements he made in these years. When he died, his emaciated body showed the ravages of the drug habit.

Years ago I became impressed with the career of an extraordinarily successful man named James Forrestal. After serving as Secretary of the Navy he was one of those responsible for the reorganization of the military forces of the United States following World War II. Because of his brilliance and capabilities he became the first Secretary of Defense and as such presided over what was at that time the most powerful military machine in the world. When he was hospitalized for an illness, however, he waited until the nurses were out of the room, walked to the window and leaped to his death.

These were successful people. They had power and wealth, influence and status. Yet success did not meet the basic needs of their lives.

But you may protest that these are not typical illustrations, for you know of successful people who have been able to cope with the circumstances of life without resorting to suicide or drugs. I am aware that not all successful people choose these alternatives. Yet of those whom I have known personally, a significant number have lived lives of "quiet desperation." They have learned that they are virtually the captives of their publics. They are not free to move about without being harassed by curiosity seekers. Indeed, a number of them have openly wished for the life they once knew when they had neither fame nor recognition.

Reportedly, Elvis Presley in his latter years found it difficult even to face his admiring fans because the publicity and lack of privacy were almost unbearable.

If success does not necessarily provide for personal fulfillment, the question remains whether the Christian who is dedicated to Jesus Christ and to obedience to God's Word can meet the challenge of success. At the outset we need to recognize, however, that not very many Christians are successful. While they have been reproached or exhorted because of this, the reason may not lie simply in their lack of diligence or commitment.

From Scripture we know that God has deliberately limited the number of Christians he has chosen to be successful. In the latter part of the first chapter of 1 Corinthians and the first part of the second chapter the Apostle Paul explains why. He says that not many wise, not many influential, and not many noble have been called by God. Then he gives two reasons why. The first is that there is a tendency, even among Christians, to glory in their accomplishments. Yet God does not want any of us to do this in his presence. The second reason is related to the Apostle's own experience with the Corinthian church. He said that he came to them in weakness and in fear and in much trembling. This was because he did not want their faith to stand in his wisdom but in God's power. Far too frequently successful Christians tend to attract others to themselves rather than to the Lord. For instance, prospective worshippers will often ask who the preacher is going to be in a particular church and then decide whether to worship there rather than in another because of the individual who is ministering. While there may be good reasons for this, often it can result in an attachment to a person rather than to the Lord. That is why the

Apostle Paul came to the Corinthian Christians as he did. He wanted to be sure their faith would stand in the power of God rather than the wisdom of men.

From Scripture we know also that God's people down the centuries have stood adversity far better than they have prosperity. That may be another reason why few of us are successful.

How then can we effectively meet the challenge of success? First of all, we must recognize just what a powerful influence it can have upon our lives. Because of its influence, success can become an end rather than simply a means to an end. This can result in a preoccupation that in time comes to ignore eternal values or spiritual qualities. From the history of God's people we know that they have turned to God far more frequently in times of tribulation than they have in periods of blessing.

Our Savior made this point in the story in Luke 16 about the rich man and Lazarus. When the rich man appealed to Abraham to send someone to his five brothers so that they would not come to the place of torment, Abraham replied that if they did not hear Moses and the prophets neither would they respond if one came back to them from the dead. Presumably the five brethren were as successful as the rich man had been. Therefore, they were as insensitive to eternal concerns or spiritual values as he had been.

From personal observation I know that this can also happen to the successful Christian. We can easily fall prey to success for its own sake and become just as preoccupied or uncomprehending as the rich man and his five brethren were.

Secondly, to meet the challenge of success we must acknowledge that all of our talents and our opportunities come from God and are not a result of our own cleverness or skill. Rather, we are but stewards of that which he has committed to our care. Thus the success that we may enjoy is because of the goodness of God rather than because of that which is inherently ours or the product of our own mastery over our destiny. A compelling illustration of this may be seen in King Hezekiah. You will recall that God granted him extraordinary deliverance from his enemies and then a most remarkable healing from a fatal disease. Yet in the account in 2 Chronicles 32 Hezekiah is described as being lifted up with pride because of what had happened to him. When visitors came to comment upon his greatness and his fame, he took the credit for all of this rather than giving glory to God. Scripture says that God left him to himself to know all that was in his heart. We should recognize how easily we can become like Hezekiah in taking the credit for that which God himself has provided for us.

Then we must accept the fact that success and accountability are linked together. The biblical statement is: "Unto whomsoever much is given, of him shall much be required" (Luke 12:48).

King Solomon is a dramatic and yet tragic illustration of this. In 1 Kings 3 there is the account of how God appeared to him in the night to ask him what he would like to receive. When Solomon asked for wisdom so that he might be able properly to govern God's people, the Lord commended him for this and promised that in addition he would receive riches and honor in abundance. All of these benefits and blessings God bestowed upon him.

Despite his extraordinary wisdom, Solomon failed to recognize that he was accountable for the resources and prestige that God had given to him. Instead, 1 Kings 11 records how that in his later years Solomon allowed his wives to turn away his heart. He became an idolater and through an obsession with self-gratification misused the advantages and blessings God had provided. Because of his failure to recognize the principle of accountability he stands as one of the most tragic figures in biblical history. As such he is an example to us. We need to remember that we shall all appear before the judgment seat of Christ and be evaluated on the basis of the deeds done in the body. As we recognize this, we shall be better able to handle success responsibly.

To meet the challenge of success, we should also understand the true nature of God's rewards. Too often, even Christians enjoy success for its own sake and in time develop a craving for more. Thus their manner of life is oriented toward that which will provide immediate gratification rather than ultimate blessing.

Our Lord spoke to this in the Sermon on the Mount. In Matthew 6 he described those who offered prayers, gave alms, or fasted in order to be seen by men. Then the Lord made this significant comment about those who acted in this way: "They have their reward."

I have speculated that the reference in Revelation about God wiping away tears from all faces may refer to the remorse some will have when they look back over their lives. Rather than recognizing the true nature of divine reward, they became preoccupied with temporal satisfaction. Like those of whom the Lord spoke, they had their reward. Then in eternity they recognized just how superficial and inadequate such rewards were. We need to have this kind of perspective so that we shall not be overcome with remorse when we stand in the presence of the Lord and at last understand the distinction between immediate gratification and his enduring commendation.

Meeting the challenge of success, however, is most significant when we recognize that God's view of success differs significantly from the popular notion. The nature of true success is suggested to us in the description of some of the individuals mentioned in Hebrews 11. To the world they must have been perceived as outcasts and failures for they wandered in the caves and dens of the earth and were destitute, afflicted, and forsaken. By no stretch of the imagination could these be considered successful in the popular sense, even though they might have been gifted and dedicated people.

Yet consider the scriptural evaluation of them, "Of whom the world was not worthy." Despite the impression that they gave to their contemporaries they were in God's sight far more worthy than the famous or the powerful of their day.

How may we meet the challenge of this kind of success? God has furnished us with a compelling example. Our Lord Jesus Christ in eternity past was God the Son. As such he was equal in power and glory with the Father. Yet he was willing to set aside all of this and to be born under the most humble of circumstances and to take upon himself the form of a servant. Even more, he subordinated himself to the death of the cross. Surely to the people of his time, including his disciples, he was an enigma. He simply did not fit their perception of success. Yet Scripture says that God highly exalted him and gave him a name that is above every other name. This then is the pattern of success that should challenge us. In their epistles, both Paul and Peter exhort us that we should follow the example of the Lord Jesus and allow his mind to be in us as we follow in his steps.

Here on campus we have had an illustration of one who saw success in these terms. John Ericksen, who was killed earlier this year, had received a significant sum of money a year or two before. Rather than simply setting this aside for his own benefit, he made out a will in which he named a number of Christian organizations as beneficiaries. When what he had done became known after his death, people found this most extraordinary. William Janz of the *Milwaukee Sentinel* wrote about this in his April 14 column. This so impressed Circuit Judge Max Raskin that he wrote to John's parents the same day to tell them how deeply moved he had been by the account of John's actions. Even as a teenager John had the divine view of success.

When I was an undergraduate, my roommate had a motto that he placed on the wall above his bed. I can recall looking across the room at that motto and being deeply influenced by it. It read, "To be in Thy will is better than success." Yet later in life I concluded that the motto might better have read, "To be in Thy will *is* success."

This is the challenge of success to which we must respond. The Lord looks for the few who are capable of handling abilities and opportunities responsibly. May it be said in the years to come that we met the challenge of success because we had the mind of Christ.

# 1979
## *A Needful Captivity*

THE JULY 21, 1978, issue of *Christianity Today* had an article by Charles Colson with the provocative title: "Religion Up, Morality Down." In this article Mr. Colson posed an important question: "How is it possible that upwards of 50 million Americans profess to have experienced the regenerative power of new life in Christ and yet are not permeating the world with the values of Christ?"

On April 18, 1979, the Carnegie Council on Policy Studies in Higher Education issued a report calling attention to signs of ethical deterioration in important aspects of academic life. The Council is to be commended for the report, even though it dealt with sensitive and controversial matters. The report enumerated a number of instances of ethical decline in academic life. For example, 80 percent of campus libraries are plagued by incidents of vandalism and theft. On some campuses up to 40 percent of the students cheat because they say this is the only way in which they can obtain good grades. More and more federally guaranteed student loans are in default, with many graduates declaring bankruptcy in order to avoid paying these off. Institutions having explicit standards of admission manipulate these in order to get more students, and use misleading advertising on the expedient basis of survival.

When these two accounts are considered together, it seems evident that something has gone wrong. If there are indeed 50 million of us in this nation who have had a transforming experience through faith in Jesus Christ, why have we not made more of an impact, particularly upon the select group of people in higher education who historically have been dedicated to ideals of honesty and integrity and to principles that support moral and ethical rectitude?

As I reflected upon this, it seemed to me that the Apostle Paul in 2 Corinthians, chapter 10, indicated long ago why such a problem exists. He said believers should not have their value structure shaped according to the standards of this world and should not wage war as the world does. The fact that he even mentions this possibility, however, suggests that there can be instances in which those who affirm biblical truth live in contradiction to it.

I believe our Lord's statements in Matthew 15 and 23 about the Pharisees also have something to say to us about this problem. In considering these passages we should remember that the Apostle Paul, being a Pharisee, was very well informed about the group to which he belonged prior to his becoming a Christian and may very well have had them in mind as he wrote to the Corinthians.

For us the term "Pharisee" has a bad connotation because of what is said in Matthew's Gospel and elsewhere. But we know from Scripture and also from Josephus and other writers that the Pharisees had commendable qualities. They sought to apply biblical truth to all of life. They were concerned that their lives be characterized by holiness and personal rectitude. However, at the time the Lord Jesus was here on earth, he found a contradiction between their affirmations and their practices. The point that he made in the Gospel of Matthew about the Pharisees was this: while in a formal sense they gave their allegiance to the Scriptures, in practice they replaced them with the traditions of men. Rather than resting their case on what God had said, they devised their own rules to govern their behavior. Thus in fact their ideals were rooted in tradition instead of Scripture; their practice conformed more to humanly devised regulations than to divine imperatives.

In the 23rd chapter of Matthew the Lord Jesus voiced his criticism this way:

> *The scribes and the Pharisees sit in Moses' seat:*
>
> *All therefore whatsoever they bid you observe, that observe and do; but do not ye after their works: for they say, and do not.*
>
> *For they bind heavy burdens and grievous to be borne, and lay them on men's shoulders; but they themselves will not move them with one of their fingers.*
>
> *But all their works they do for to be seen of men.*
>
> [*Matt. 23:2-5*].

Then he gave illustrations of what he had in mind. To show how the Pharisees were saying one thing and doing another, he cited their response to the commandment, "Honor thy father and thy mother." The Pharisees affirmed this, but then circumvented it by the use of clever hermeneutics. On this basis a person could say to his parents that what he should have given to them had been dedicated to the Lord, thus avoiding a responsibility clearly enunciated in Scripture.

Similarly, our Lord's illustration of the Pharisee and the publican addressed the issue of inner motivation. The man who boasted that he fasted twice in the week and gave tithes of all that he possessed deliberately chose to stand in a public place and to voice his prayer audibly for the purpose of justifying himself before his hearers and his viewers.

There is, I believe, a disturbing parallel between the Pharisees of Jesus' day and the evangelicalism to which so many of us have given our allegiance. Like the Pharisees, we are dedicated to the acceptance of God's truth and its application to life. We speak of this as the integration of faith and learning, for we desire that all we do might be informed by the teachings of the Scriptures. Specifically, we have been concerned about

116

holiness of life. We have thought it essential to live a life that in character and activity would be different from that of a disobedient world. This also is the conviction of literally scores of thousands of dedicated Christians who call themselves evangelicals.

Yet today within evangelicalism there are efforts to take the unambiguous statements of Holy Scripture and interpret these on the basis of today's cultural notions. One illustration of this is in the area of human sexuality. There is a determined endeavor, through the use of hermeneutical devices, to manipulate precise scriptural commandments so that they no longer mean what they say.

Other illustrations could be given, *both* from the so-called establishment evangelicals and the countercultural evangelicals, of how an accommodation to the present culture influenced the way Scripture is being viewed. Inevitably this expresses itself in actual practice.

I am grieved when I see in my own life and the lives of my fellow evangelicals the preaching of self-denial but the practice of self-indulgence; the preaching that eternal values are of the greatest consequence but the practice that temporal needs are of the most immediate and highest priority; the preaching that one should love God and have a concern for one's neighbors, but the practice of ignoring the clear statement of our Lord Jesus Christ when he said, "If you love me, keep my commandments"; the preaching that we should prefer one another in humility of mind but the practice of character assassination and the building of one's own reputation at the expense of others, with exploitation of those who most need our ministry.

One would also have to say that within the fellowship of evangelicals there has too often been the doing of our deeds to be seen of men. Evangelicalism is in danger of falling prey to the cult of the dynamic personality by following individuals who make a practice of calling attention to themselves. Today within the evangelical community we have groups dedicated to the task of image-building, a phrase that has always caused me disquiet because it suggests manipulation. Too often it implies the creation of an impression that may not be entirely accurate, the employment of the rationalization that the end justifies the means, and the achievement of a result that far too frequently exalts the personality of the individual rather than the character of our Lord Jesus Christ himself.

Now when one looks at these things, whether in the historic, biblical example of the Pharisees or in the contemporary illustrations that can be found within our own fellowship, one is moved to ask, "Why?" Our Lord Jesus Christ has given us an answer, and I urge you to recognize it as a basic truth and to remember it always. The Savior said, in effect, that even though there could be formal commitment to biblical truth there could also be within the heart an opposition to that truth. Furthermore, the heart attitude inevitably will manifest itself. In the last analysis there is no way in which one can prevent the attitude of the heart from eventually becoming dominant in the pattern of life. You can say that you believe the great creeds as I do. But unless there is a heart commitment to that affirmation, the signing will soon become but a charade. There will be no enduring significance to our formal affirmations if we fail to address the basic issue of our heart attitude. Surely, we know this. But some of us say that we love the Lord but in practice contradict that affirmation. It seems to me the Savior directly addressed this issue. Thus, if there is in our inner being a counterprinciple, it will prevail with great loss to us because of the conflict set up between what is objectively true and what subjectively is held as normative.

It is not my purpose, however, simply to emphasize my concern about this dilemma, because there is a solution to it. In Paul's statement in 2 Corinthians 10, he specified it. The way in which we are to have our standards set and the way in which we are to wage war in this conflict is to be "casting down imaginations, and every high thing that exalts itself against the knowledge of God." That is the first principle. And the

118

second is—"bringing into captivity every thought to the obedience of Christ." On the one hand, we are consciously and deliberately to reject those things that come to us in our quiet and reflective moments, when we ponder them in our hearts. These, he says, are to be cast down. Then, the thoughts that we have are to be led into subjection in obedience to Jesus Christ.

Paul began this tenth chapter by describing the attitude of our Lord Jesus. This is the attitude that you and I should have in obeying this Scripture. He appealed to the Corinthians this way: "I. . .beseech you by the meekness and the gentleness of Christ." You may say, "Why meekness? Meekness is weakness." But it is not so in the biblical sense. Think of Moses. Scripture says he was one of the meekest of all the men that lived upon the earth, but do you remember the description of him in the Book of Exodus, when he came down from the mountain and saw the disobedience of God's people? He ground the golden calf to powder, put it in the water, made the Israelites drink that water and forthrightly imposed judgment upon God's disobedient people. That was not weakness!

What then is meekness? How could our Lord Jesus Christ himself say, "I am meek and lowly in heart and you shall find rest unto your souls." Meekness is what Moses sought to exemplify by voluntarily subordinating himself to the commands of God and by being zealous always to protect the glory of God. A meek person is one who will set aside all other concerns that God's glory might be advanced and his commands obeyed. So the Apostle appeals to you and to me on the basis of the meekness of Christ.

What shall we say then about the gentleness of Christ? In the scriptural sense gentleness means tractability, or being able to say, "I dedicate myself to God's glory. I subordinate myself to God's commandments." But this must be fleshed out in experience. That is why Paul appeals to us, on the basis of the gentleness of Christ, to be willing actually to do what we affirm.

119

The meekness and gentleness of which I have been speaking have a compelling illustration. Let us imagine that we are standing at a crossroads, with one road leading into the Garden of Eden and the other into the Garden of Gethsemane. In our imagination we approach the Garden of Eden, and there we hear a conversation going on. A creature who looks like an angel of light is talking to a lady, and he says to her, "Has God really said this? God knows that the day in which you eat of this fruit, you will not surely die. Instead, you will become as gods, knowing good and evil."

Many an evangelical is at just such a crossroads where he may be lured down the road to the Garden of Eden. What is the attraction? Exactly what the Lord Jesus and the Apostle Paul declared. There is the temptation to establish one's own criteria in the area of morality and ethics, good and evil.

The other garden is the Garden of Gethsemane. In our mind's eye we see there three figures asleep while one figure is bent in prayer. He is obviously under great emotional stress because, as we draw near, we see enormous drops of perspiration on his brow and dropping off his chin and beard. They look to us like great drops of blood falling down. As we come closer, we hear from his twisted lips and out of his agonized heart these words, "O my Father, if it be possible, let this cup pass from me: nevertheless not as I will, but as thou wilt. . . . O my Father, if this cup may not pass away from me, except I drink it, thy will be done." Here we see illustrated the meekness and the gentleness of Christ.

Today in a very real way we stand at the crossroads. From one garden we hear the clever blandishments of the tempter who as an angel of light says in effect to us, "Formulate your ideals in accordance with the traditions of men. Let your lifestyle be on the basis of the rules that you establish for yourself. Then you can have self-fulfillment, self-realization, self-gratification." But from the other garden these words echo in our ears, "Not my will, but yours be done."

In this context let us respond to the Apostle's exhortation.

By the dynamic power of the blessed Holy Spirit that is in our lives, let us resolve by the grace of God to lead every thought —the thought that would advance our own egotism, that would indulge disobedience in our hearts, that would encourage indifference to the clear statements of Scripture—captive to the obedience of Christ.

I urge you to accept this needful captivity and make it your own. Amen.

# May the Mind of
# Christ My Savior

Singing hymns together has long been traditional for both congregation and graduates at the annual Baccalaureate Service of Wheaton College. However, in 1968 the printed program carried the words of the beautiful hymn written by Kate B. Wilkinson entitled "May the Mind of Christ My Savior." Then serving in his third year as president of the college, Dr. Hudson T. Armerding selected this hymn because of the meaningful content of its words for all committed believers—but particularly for young people, who have so much potential. Every year since then, with concurrence by the officers of each graduating class, this hymn has appeared in the printed program for the Baccalaureate Service. It has been sung immediately following the president's message—his last to the gathered group in the College Chapel. All voices, congregation and graduates, sing the first three stanzas with organ accompaniment; but the last three stanzas are sung a cappella as a response by the graduates. These are the words that have stirred the hearts of many on those occasions:

*May the mind of Christ, my Savior,*
*Live in me from day to day,*
*By His love and pow'r controlling*
*All I do and say.*

*May the Word of God dwell richly*
*In my heart from hour to hour,*
*So that all may see I triumph*
*Only through His pow'r.*

*May the peace of God, my Father,*
*Rule my life in everything,*
*That I may be calm to comfort*
*Sick and sorrowing.*

*May the love of Jesus fill me,*
*As the waters fill the sea;*
*Him exalting, self abasing,*
*This is victory.*

*May I run the race before me,*
*Strong and brave to face the foe,*
*Looking only unto Jesus*
*As I onward go.*

*May His beauty rest upon me*
*As I seek the lost to win,*
*And may they forget the channel,*
*Seeing only Him. Amen.*

# Charge to the Bride and Groom

*Over the years, Dr. Armerding has been asked to preside over the marriage ceremonies of many young Christian couples, often just after commencement activities have been completed. Although each wedding has had its own special character and unique spiritual quality, Dr. Armerding's biblical exhortations on these occasions have been motivated by common concerns, and thus have assumed a certain form. Many have requested a transcription of these ceremonies. Here then is a condensation of that material*
    *—Dr. Armerding's Charge to the Bride and Groom.*

DEARLY BELOVED, we are assembled here in the presence of God, to join this couple in holy marriage, which is instituted of God, regulated by his commandments, blessed by our Lord Jesus Christ, and to be held in honor among all men. Let us therefore reverently remember that God has established and sanctified marriage for the welfare and happiness of mankind. Our Savior has declared that a man shall forsake his father and mother and cleave unto his wife. By his apostles, he has instructed those who enter into this relation to cherish a mutual esteem and love; to bear with each other's infirmities and weaknesses; to comfort each other in sickness, trouble, and sorrow; in honesty and industry to provide for each other and for their household in temporal things; to pray for and encourage each other in the things which pertain to God; and to live together as heirs of the grace of life.

Hear now what the Scriptures teach as touching the duty of husbands to their wives and wives to their husbands:

Wives, submit to your husbands as to the Lord. For the husband is the head of the wife as Christ is the head of the Church, his body, of which he is the Savior. Now as the Church submits to Christ, so also wives should submit to their husbands in everything.

Husbands, love your wives, just as Christ loved the Church and gave himself up for her to make her holy, cleansing her by the washing with water through the word, and to present her to himself as a radiant Church, without stain or wrinkle or any other blemish, but holy and blameless. In this same way, husbands ought to love their wives as their own bodies. He who loves his wife loves himself. After all, no one ever hated his own body, but he feeds and cares for it, just as Christ does the Church—for we are members of his body. "For this cause shall a man leave his father and mother, and shall be joined to his wife, and they two shall be one flesh." This is a profound mystery—but I am talking about Christ and the Church. However, each one of you also must love his wife as he loves himself, and the wife must respect her husband.

### Charge to the Groom

To you, the husband, has been committed the high and holy privilege of spiritual leadership in the home. You are directed by the Word of God to exercise that leadership in such a manner as to validate your fitness for a place of responsibility among the Lord's people. This will require of you the highest qualities of integrity and spiritual reality and an obedience to the lordship of Christ that is absolute and unconditional. Let it be said of you that your wife finds in you this excellence of performance and example in your most quiet moments as well as in your occasions of public ministry.

It is your privilege also to be the provider and protector of the home. The Scripture makes plain that those who do not fulfill this trust have denied their faith. Conversely, those who do honor this responsibility exhibit to society at large as well as to the household of faith the quality of their fidelity. Moreover, let this provision incorporate the emotional and spiritual security that it is the husband's unique privilege to provide.

Above all, remember that your love for your wife is to be akin to that which Christ had for his Church. As you have known personally of this love in your Christian experience, you are to manifest its same characteristics and qualities toward the one you have chosen to be your wife. And may her response to this love of yours be your highest reward.

### Charge to the Bride

Now to you, the wife, has been committed the unique and important ministry of being a helpmeet for your husband. Even as he bestows his love upon you and makes provision for your physical, emotional, and spiritual needs, so you are to love and cherish him in such a way as to provide for his utmost fulfillment and encouragement in his life and ministry. To you also is given the privilege of guiding the home, a responsibility that will utilize the talents and abilities the Lord has bestowed upon you.

In your role as helpmeet you also will serve the Lord and your husband best by your unswerving devotion to the will and purpose of God, as evidenced by your integrity and faithfulness in the marriage bond. In so doing you will be a strength and an inspiration to your husband and to all who observe you as a loving and faithful wife.

As you give your husband your love, respect, and support, he will, together with you, evidence a completeness that will surely illustrate the purpose a loving heavenly Father had in instituting marriage.

*Charge to the Bride and Groom*

To you both has been given the holy privilege of demonstrating to the world about you in a tangible way that union that exists between Christ and his Church. The Christian home stands today as an eloquent witness to a disintegrating culture that there is strength and stability to be found in God's holy ordinance. Be well assured that the love and devotion you have for one another will provide a needed inspiration to those who have tested the alternatives and found them wanting. Let your life together be this kind of a compelling witness. The favor of our heavenly Father will rest upon it, the fragrance of the presence of Christ will hallow it, and the fruitfulness of the blessed Holy Spirit will constantly characterize it.

Whom God has joined together let no man put asunder.

*The Lord bless you and keep you*
*The Lord make his face to shine upon you and be gracious unto*
*   you*
*The Lord lift up the light of his countenance upon you and give*
*   you peace*
*Through Jesus Christ our Lord.*

*Amen.*